Wow.

Our Amazing Planet

Barnabas
in
Schools

Barnabas for Children® is a registered word mark and the logo is a registered device mark of The Bible Reading Fellowship.

Text and illustrations copyright © A Rocha 2013
The author asserts the moral right
to be identified as the author of this work

Published by
The Bible Reading Fellowship
15 The Chambers, Vineyard
Abingdon OX14 3FE
United Kingdom
Tel: +44 (0)1865 319700
Email: enquiries@brf.org.uk
Website: www.brf.org.uk
BRF is a Registered Charity

ISBN 978 0 85746 249 7

First published 2013
10 9 8 7 6 5 4 3 2 1 0

Acknowledgments
Unless otherwise stated, scripture quotations are taken from the Contemporary English Version of the Bible published by HarperCollins Publishers, copyright © 1991, 1992, 1995 American Bible Society.

Scripture quotations taken from the Holy Bible, New International Version, copyright © 1973, 1978, 1984 by International Bible Society, are used by permission of Hodder & Stoughton Publishers, a member of the Hachette Livre Group UK. All rights reserved. 'NIV' is a registered trademark of International Bible Society. UK trademark number 1448790.

Scriptures marked (NLT) are taken from the Holy Bible, New Living Translation, copyright © 1996, 2004. Used by permission of Tyndale House Publishers, Inc., Wheaton, Illinois 60189. All rights reserved.

Photographs and Illustrations
Cover: back, top left to right – Michael Day, Creative Commons; A Rocha; BMM Explorer, Creative Commons; A Rocha. Bottom left to right: A Rocha; Peter Edin, Creative Commons; Anne Toal, Creative Commons; Norman Crowson. Front – snail, ladybird, bird feeders: David Chandler; toucan: Brian Gratwicke, Creative Commons; red kite: Des Haslam; rainbow: Mike Baird, Creative Commons; clownfish: Bendus, Creative Commons; juniper planting, A Rocha; elephants, Kathryn Bedford; bee, dormouse: Norman Crowson; coral: Benjamin Cowburn, A Rocha; frog: Ryan Cozie, Creative Commons.

Inside pages: pages 6, 13, 18, 23, 24 (numbers 4 and 10), 27, 30, 31, 50, 53, 54, 58, 64, 67 (mangrove), 69, 74, 84, 85, 86 (Asian elephants), 87: A Rocha; pages 11, 12, 21, 34, 41, 43, 45, 70, 81, 88, 89: Ray and Corinne Burrows/Beehive Illustration; pages 20, 25, 26, 29 (ladybird): David Chandler; page 24 (numbers 1, 2, 3, 5, 6, 7, 8, 9): Norman Crowson; pages 28, 57 (dormouse): Norman Crowson; page 29 (wasp): Quinet, Creative Commons; page 48: iStockphoto/Thinkstock; page 57 (Atlantic cod): Peter Edin, Creative Commons; page 61: Michael Day, Creative Commons; pages 62, 63 (coral): Benjamin Cowburn, A Rocha; page 63 (parrotfish): BMM Explorer, Creative Commons; page 67 (cacao): Ever. Jean, Creative Commons; page 73: Colin Towner; page 86 (African elephants): Kathryn Bedford; page 87 (Golden-rumped elephant shrew): Galen Rathbun.

The paper used in the production of this publication was supplied by mills that source their raw materials from sustainably managed forests. Soy-based inks were used in its printing and the laminate film is biodegradable.

A catalogue record for this book is available from the British Library

Printed in Singapore by Craft Print International Ltd

Wow!

Our Amazing Planet

A cross-curricular conservation resource for RE teachers

David Chandler

Acknowledgments

There are quite a few people to say thank you to:

Steve Hughes and Glenys Hulme at A Rocha UK for giving me the opportunity to write *Wow! Our Amazing Planet*; Glenys for her ideas and many hours of research; Glenys again, and Julia Major, an A Rocha volunteer from Hungary, for the illustrations; A Rocha UK's education team for their ideas that we have used here; Dave Bookless for allowing himself to form part of the content and for making sure that the theology isn't off-track; and Herb Enmarch-Williams for his input.

Thanks too to the photographers, filmmakers and PowerPoint creators who have contributed to this book and the online resources that support it. Particular thanks are due to Norman Crowson, who gave more photos than most. You can see more of his work at http://normancrowsonphotography.co.uk.

At BRF, thanks to Olivia Warburton and Lisa Cherrett for sharpening my words with their editing skills, and to all of the wordsmiths and designers who helped to turn our raw material into this finished product.

Finally, as ever, thanks to my family for their support throughout.

Important information

Photocopy permission

The Copyright Licensing Agency (CLA)

Contents

Foreword

I became a botanist, ecologist and conservationist because of a good school teacher and encouragement from various relations and friends at a very young age. *Wow! Our Amazing Planet!* is a wonderful teaching resource, full of information about the wonders of creation, the abuse of creation by humans, and some of the solutions towards stopping the destruction. It is a vital resource for you because it is directed towards a future generation of conservationists and protectors of creation.

The favourite class of my young grandchildren is forest school. When I see how much they learn about nature in the local area around an urban school in Plymouth, I am delighted that their teacher so effectively puts to use a small area of woodland. In this resource you will find helpful information about common birds, insects and animals, and many activities for your pupils.

Written from a Christian point of view, this is a book that encourages hope. I urge you to use it to its fullest extent—to say 'Wow!' about the amazing facts it contains and to stimulate some of your class to become the naturalists and conservationists upon whom our future and the future of our planet must be built.

Sir Ghillean Prance FRS
Former Director of Kew Gardens

Introduction

This is a resource for anyone who wants to teach creation care in Key Stage 1 or Key Stage 2 RE lessons. Religious Education promotes the values of truth, justice, respect for all and care of the environment, and helps children to develop a sense of appreciation and wonder at the world in which they live. *Wow! Our Amazing Planet* supports this learning 'about religion and from religion', and also provides cross-curricular links to literacy (creative writing), science, geography and citizenship/PSHE. It has been produced by Barnabas in Schools for the Bible Reading Fellowship (BRF) in collaboration with A Rocha, a Christian conservation organisation that works in 19 countries around the world. You can find out more about A Rocha at www.arocha.org. You can find out more about BRF at www.brf.org.uk.

Wow! Our Amazing Planet will help you to understand and explore some of the things that the Bible has to say about God and creation, about Jesus and creation, and about humanity's role as part of creation. We hope that you find it a really helpful and useful resource, and that if this thinking is new to you, it gives you some fresh insights into the Christian faith.

How to use this resource

Wow! Our Amazing Planet is divided into six sections. These are in a logical order and we recommend that you use them sequentially. You won't have time to do everything that we suggest, but do try to include the key messages from each section. To support each message, look through the book and find the approaches and activities that you think will work best with your class. The six sections are:

1. **Yes, it is amazing!** This introductory section reminds us that the planet we live on really is amazing.
2. **My wonderful, wild, local area.** Use this section to open the eyes of the children you are working with to the wonders of the wildlife that lives alongside us. We don't have to travel to faraway places to encounter some remarkable creatures.
3. **Whose world?** This section looks at the biblical account of creation and the story of Noah's ark.

Then it focuses on two Christians with a passion for creation—a famous historic person (St Francis) and a less well-known contemporary person (Dave Bookless).

4. **Whose fault?** Our track record of looking after creation is by no means perfect. This section highlights a range of examples. It includes information about species, habitats and climate change, and also looks at why we should save species.
5. **Who cares?** Section 5 is more positive. It talks about the role of governments and individuals. It encourages engagement with the political process and suggests some practical things that you and your class can do.
6. **Is there hope for our world?** The final section is even more positive. It paints the big picture of the hope that Christians have in Jesus and tells some good news stories from A Rocha and from the wider conservation world.

This resource contains a large amount of material. It includes:

- Background information to save you time and give you confidence. If the content is new to you, we hope that it will make you look more expert than you are! There is information about wildlife, wild places and conservation issues, and about what the Bible has to say.
- Ready-made stories that you can tell straight off the page.
- Lots of activity ideas, with an indication of whether they will work with Key Stage 1 or Key Stage 2, and some suggestions for Key Stage 2 extension activities. Don't see these indications as a straitjacket, though: you know your class better than we do. If you think it will work, give it a go.
- Pages that you can copy and use with your class.
- Links to PowerPoint presentations, colour photographs, downloadable copiable materials and films that you can use to deliver this material.
- Suggested websites, particularly for film clips.
- Suggestions of other resources that you might find helpful.

We haven't been able to include colour photographs in the book. Many of the creatures and places look their best in colour, however, so we have created an online photo gallery for you to use. You can find it at www.barnabasinschools.org.uk/9780857462497/.

Safety

You know the children you teach and your school's risk assessment procedures better than we do. Please take all appropriate steps to ensure the safety of the children you are working with when using any of the ideas in this book.

Bible references

Bible references are shown throughout this book with chapter and verse numbers separated by a colon. So, for example, to look up Genesis 1:31, first find chapter 1 and then verse 31.

Yes, it is amazing!

We live on a planet that, as far as anyone knows, is the only planet anywhere that supports life. In our solar system, it's one of eight planets that move around the sun. The sun is 150 million kilometres away and we move around it once a year at an average speed of 30km/second. That's about 67,500 miles per hour. If we were too near the sun, the earth would be too hot for life to survive. If we were too far away, it would be too cold.

While we are travelling around the sun, the earth is spinning. It spins around once every 24 hours on an axis that is a bit off-centre. That's what gives us our seasons. And while we are going around in circles travelling around the sun, the moon is going around us.

The earth is made of rock and is more or less spherical in shape. It has a diameter of about 13,000km and weighs 59-with-20-zeroes tonnes. Seventy per cent of the earth is covered in water, with the deepest ocean going down eleven km. The sea is deeper than the mountains are high. Mount Everest, our highest mountain, is nearly nine km high.

No one has found any other planets that have anywhere near the amount of oxygen that we have in our air. It really is an amazing planet. And the life on this planet is amazing too. This is a world with rushing streams, meandering rivers, beautiful lakes, crashing waterfalls and mighty oceans. There are bogs, swamps and marshes; forests that are hot and humid and forests that are cold; flat places; hills and mountains; grasslands and deserts; towns and cities—and, at the last count, over seven billion people. You're one of them.

No one knows exactly how many species of plant and animal you share this planet with. There are creatures too small to see without a microscope, and there are huge whales swimming in the oceans. There are animals with no legs, two legs, four legs, six legs, eight legs, ten legs, 14 legs and hundreds of legs. Birds with feathers, mammals with fur, and fish and reptiles with scales. Animals that run, jump, sing, dance, swim, burrow and fly. Beautiful creatures and creatures that don't look so good. Brightly coloured beasts and brilliantly camouflaged ones. Trees that live for thousands of years and a fungus that could cover more than 1600 football pitches.

Most of them haven't been named yet. New species are still being discovered. So far, scientists have given names to about two million different species. They have a long way to go: there could be another eight million out there.

Yes, it is amazing. In fact, the Bible says that when God had finished creating the earth, he took a look at his handiwork and described it as 'very good' (Genesis 1:31). In the Psalms, David writes, 'The earth and everything on it belong to the Lord' (Psalm 24:1). So the Bible says that God made it very good—he made it amazing—and it all belongs to him. But it also says that he has given humankind the job of looking after it.

Read on to find out more about this amazing world and what Christianity has to say about our relationship with it and God's relationship with it.

Activities

  Amazing place

Remind your class just how amazing our planet is. You could do this by:

- Using a PowerPoint presentation. We've provided one, called 'Our Amazing Planet'. You can find it at www.barnabasinschools.org.uk/9780857462497/.
- Using the facts on page 9, perhaps with others that you know or can find.
- Watching part of a DVD—something from a David Attenborough series, perhaps.

Then try this:

  Amazing adjectives

Ask the children to think of adjectives that could be used to describe wild places and wild plants and animals. The whole class could do this together, with you writing the words on the whiteboard, or you could ask the children to work in small groups.

 Amazing colouring

Ask the class to draw and colour an amazing landscape, seascape or piece of wildlife. They can do this from scratch, or, if you prefer, use one of the templates provided. If they do their own drawing, you could make it huge, and have the whole class contributing to one fantastic picture. They could even produce a collage. Use books or the internet to find out what the habitats and creatures look like if you need to.

We have included two templates on pages 11 and 12. One is a British woodland with the following animals in it:

- Butterfly
- Stag beetle
- Ladybird
- Bumblebee
- Ants
- Great spotted woodpecker
- Jay
- Blackbird
- Badger
- Squirrel
- Rabbit
- Fox

The other is a piece of African savannah. It includes:

- Lion
- Hippopotamus
- Snake
- Zebra
- Stork
- Giraffe
- Rhinoceros
- Antelope
- Hyena

 Amazing facts

Ask the children to do some independent research. Ask them to find one amazing fact about a plant, animal or wild place to share with the rest of the class or in an assembly. They can use books or the internet, and work singly or in pairs.

My wonderful, wild, local area

The children in your class might think that exciting wildlife is only found in exotic faraway places, and that the only way they can experience it is second-hand, on TV. It's not true! Wherever you live, there is wildlife nearby. OK, probably not whales, tigers, pythons or lemurs—but the fact is, not far from where you're sitting, there are some remarkable creatures.

This section introduces children to some of the creatures that live nearby. We've included some facts to help you communicate the wonder of these animals to the class, focusing your attention on birds and minibeasts, which are the animals you are most likely to encounter. You're very likely to find creatures that we haven't written about here, too. Once you've worked out what they are, encourage the children to do some research to see what they can find out about them. There's a list of resources on page 91 that you might find useful.

Use the information and activities in this section to enthuse your class about wildlife. The Bible says that these are God's creatures, and that they look to him for their food. Here's a quote from Psalm 104:24 and 27:

Our Lord, by your wisdom you made so many things; the whole earth is covered with your living creatures… All of these depend on you to provide them with food.

The birdy bits

Gulls

Please don't call them seagulls—you can see them a long way inland. At school, if you see gulls, they will probably be flying over or just loafing around on the school playing field. It's not unusual to see more than one species in the same flock. Here's some information about three of the gull species that you might see. Use a bird book or the RSPB website (www.rspb.org.uk) to help you work out which ones you are looking at—or just enjoy them.

Black-headed gull

- These gulls have a dark head only when they are in their breeding plumage, and even then it's brown, not black. When they are not in their breeding plumage, they have a dark smudge behind the eye.
- When they are flying, look for the white line along the front edge of the wing.
- They like eating worms. The gulls tap the ground with their feet. The worms mistake this for the noise of rainfall, come up to the surface and get eaten.

Common gull

- Despite its name, this bird is not that common. The word 'common' used to be used to describe something that was relatively featureless. Maybe that's why they're called common gulls.
- Common gulls also use the foot-tapping trick to bring out the worms.

Herring gull

- This is the big, grey-backed gull with a red spot on its beak that you see at the seaside. But you can see them inland too.
- The red spot on the beak gives herring gull chicks something to aim at. They peck the spot on their parent's beak to make it clear that they want some food.

Pigeons

There are three types of pigeon that you are likely to notice. The big fat ones with a white patch on the neck and a white bar across the wing (you can see it when they fly) are wood pigeons. The smaller, pinky-brown ones with a black collar are collared doves. You might see feral pigeons too. These are about the same size as a collared dove but come in a variety of colours—grey, brown, black and white—and patterns. Some of them are chequered or mottled. These are the ones you see at railway stations.

Pigeon propaganda

- Young pigeons are called 'squabs'. When they are a bit older they're called 'squeakers'.
- Squabs are fed on pigeon milk. It is made on the adults' throat lining and both parents produce it.
- Pigeon milk looks like pale yellow cottage cheese and is loaded with protein and fat. The adult regurgitates it to feed it to the squabs.
- To drink, most birds tip their head up and let the water trickle down their throat. Not pigeons! They poke their beak in and suck up the water.

Feral pigeon

- The wild ancestor of the feral pigeon is the rock dove. Rock doves were domesticated a long time ago, perhaps about 8000BC, to provide food for people. Feral pigeons are descendants of domesticated rock doves that have 'gone wild'.
- If there's enough food, feral pigeons breed pretty well all year round, laying eggs up to five times a year.
- Some people keep pigeons and race them, to see which ones find their way home the quickest over a long distance. Sometimes racing pigeons stop for a rest on the way home, so you might see one in the school grounds. It will have a ring on its leg. The ring won't have a join—it will be a complete circle. If you find a racing pigeon, visit www.rpra.org to find out what to do.
- Pigeons have been used to carry messages for thousands of years. In 1896 a pigeon post service was started in New Zealand. Pigeons carried messages in the First and Second World Wars: some of them even won medals for bravery!

Collared dove

- This bird is very common now, but it hasn't always been, at least not in the UK. In the 1930s, collared doves started to expand their range from Turkey. No one is sure why. They arrived in Britain in the 1950s, bred here for the first time in 1955, and now they are almost everywhere.
- A collared dove's coo has three syllables with equal emphasis: 'coo coo coo'. Have a listen.

Wood pigeon

- A wood pigeon's coo has five syllables, with a different rhythm and emphasis than a collared dove's. Have a listen to these, too. Try to match their sound to a memorable phrase. 'My leg hurts Bet-ty' is one option for the wood pigeon. Do the same for collared doves.
- Wood pigeons also clatter their wings. You might hear this if you accidentally disturb one in a tree or bush and it comes crashing out.
- Try to see a wood pigeon's display flight. They do a rollercoaster flight with a wingclap at the top of the climb. Then they stop flapping and drop down.
- You could take a look at 'Pesky Pigeons' on Bill Oddie's 'Top 10 Birds'. It can be found at www.bbc.co.uk/programmes/p007yg9n and lasts about 90 seconds.

Pied wagtail

This bird is often seen around school playgrounds and it's easy to see how it got its name—it's pied (which means black and white), and it wags its tail.

Wagtail wonders

- Wagtails are minibeast-munchers. When they are feeding on the ground, wagging their tail probably disturbs potential prey and helps the wagtail find something to eat. Their tail helps them steer when they are chasing insects in mid-air, too.
- If you live in London you might have heard of the Chiswick Flyover, a well-known road. It's a good name for this bird too—pied wagtails fly over going 'chis-ick'. They do this to find out if there is another pied wagtail feeding nearby. If there is, the feeding bird calls back and the one flying over carries on flying.
- Pied wagtails are famous for roosting (sleeping) with lots of other pied wagtails. You might see them gathering as the light fades. Supermarket car parks can be good places to look. The birds meet up and then fly to their roost site, in bushes and trees, or perhaps in a wetland. There could be hundreds nestling down for the night in the same area.
- Watch a pied wagtail walking and running. Watch what it does with its tail and head. Then see if the children can move in a similar way.

Blackbird

Most people can identify a male blackbird, especially in the summer. It's black, with yellow rings around its eyes and a lovely yellow bill. Its bill gets darker at the end of summer. Don't mix them up with starlings. Starlings walk—they don't hop like blackbirds. Starlings have shorter tails and, especially in the winter, pale spots.

Female blackbirds are actually brown, with some streaks on the breast.

Brilliant blackbirds

- A male blackbird singing is one of the sounds of summer. They sing a lovely, tuneful, mellow song, from a chimney pot near you, perhaps. Take a listen. You could ask the children to try to describe the sound. Their alarm call is quite different—it's a harsh rattle. It's not beautiful but it does the job. You can hear a blackbird singing on the bird pages of the RSPB website (www.rspb.org.uk). Look under 'Birds & wildlife', then 'Birds by name'.
- Blackbirds may rear two or three broods of young every year. Each brood normally contains three to five eggs, so the parents could raise up to 15 young blackbirds in one season.
- Watch a blackbird looking for food on the grass. It will stop with its head on one side. It's listening for moving worms. Blackbirds like eating worms—you might be able to watch a tug of war as a blackbird heaves a worm out of the ground before gobbling it down.
- There are some video clips of blackbirds on www.arkive.org. Go to 'Birds', then 'Explore all birds', and search for 'Blackbird'. Make sure you look at the right one: *Turdus merula*.

Robin

If there is one bird that everyone in your class will be able to identify, this is probably it. The only pitfall might be young robins. When they are first out of the nest, they don't have the orangey breast of the adult bird. Six or seven weeks later they grow some new feathers and acquire the 'red' breast that we expect a robin to have.

Read about robins

- Male and female robins look alike—they both have a rusty-red breast.
- Unlike most birds, robins can be heard singing in any season. And, also unlike most birds, the male and the female sing. Normally, it's the males that do the singing. Males and females sing in the autumn to defend a feeding area. Their song sounds sadder at this time of the year.
- Robins sing at night, too. There's a song called 'A nightingale sang in Berkeley Square', but in reality it's more likely to be a robin.
- Robins are feisty little birds and are not always as nice as they look. The territory holder's song will usually warn other robins off. When that fails, a robin will use its red breast in a threat display. Then, if the intruder still doesn't go away, things get physical. They fight, sometimes to the death.
- Once upon a time, robins followed wild boars that were snuffling around looking for food. The snuffling boars unearthed and disturbed mini-beasts that were easy pickings for the robins. When robins come close to gardeners, they're doing something similar—they think you're a pig!
- We associate robins with Christmas. This is because the first postmen wore bright red waistcoats and were known as 'robins'. That may be why you sometimes see robins on Christmas cards with letters in their beaks.
- There are some short video clips of robins on www. arkive.org. Go to 'Birds', then 'Explore all birds', and search for 'Robin'. Make sure you look at the right one: *Erithacus rubecula*.

Wren

The wren is a tiny brown bird with a poking-up tail, but it's not the UK's smallest bird. You could ask your class to find out what is the smallest. It's the goldcrest, which is quite common, or the firecrest, which isn't very common. These are both 9cm long and weigh about 6g. A wren is 10cm long and weighs 10g. That's about the same weight as a £1 coin.

Read about wrens

- They may be tiny, but they have a very big voice. A wren's song is loud—you can hear one singing on the bird pages of the RSPB website (www.rspb.org. uk). Look under 'Birds & wildlife', then 'Birds by name'.
- It's hard for small birds to keep warm in the winter. To help themselves survive, wrens roost with other wrens, sometimes in nestboxes. There's a record of 63 wrens coming out of one nestbox. That must have been cosy!
- A male wren builds more than one nest, sometimes as many as five. The female inspects all the nests and decides which one she wants to use.
- You might not see them very often, but the wren is the commonest bird that breeds in Britain. We have over eight million wren territories. They live in woods and on farmland, heaths and moors. You often see them in gardens.

Blue tit

Not everyone is sure how to tell a blue tit from a great tit. The blue tit is smaller—it's not as great! It has a blue cap and a black eyestripe. A blue tit weighs a lot less than a great tit. This means that it can feed from smaller twigs than its heavier relative can.

Blue tit titbits

- Blue tits are inquisitive. If you put up a new bird feeder, a blue tit may be the first bird to investigate it.
- Blue tits are acrobats. They will even hang upside down to get at food.
- Holes in trees are a blue tit's natural nest site. Nest boxes are like man-made holes in trees, and blue tits often use them.
- Blue tits eat minibeasts, seeds and nuts… and they drink nectar—well, sometimes, anyway. A nectar-feeding blue tit will pull off the flower and peck its way in or poke its bill into the flower so that it can reach the sugary nectar.
- In the UK, blue tits normally lay just one clutch of eggs in a season. They lay seven to 13 eggs, so there could be a lot of hungry beaks to feed.
- There are some short video clips of blue tits on www.arkive.org. Go to 'Birds', then 'Explore all birds', and search for 'Blue tit'.

Great tit

This is the blue tit's bigger relative. It has a black head with big white cheek patches, and a much more obvious black stripe down its front.

Great tit titbits

- The great tit is the 'teacher bird'. Its song sounds a bit like 'tea-cher tea-cher tea-cher teach'. Great tits make lots of different noises, though. Birdwatchers say that if they're in a wood and hear a noise they don't recognise, it's usually a great tit.
- Take a look at a great tit's belly stripe. This is wider on the males; and the wider it is, the better. A wider stripe makes a male more attractive to the females.
- A nest full of young great tits needs a lot of cater-pillars. At one nest, over two weeks, food was delivered 12,685 times.

Starling

This is another bird that's familiar to most people, but starlings are nowhere near as common as they used to be. In fact, their numbers have gone down so much that they were put on the UK's red list of Birds of Conservation Concern in 2002 and 2009.

Stunning starlings

- Starlings look black from a distance, but up close you can see lovely green and purple iridescence. These are handsome birds.
- In spring you can tell males from females by the colour at the base of the beak. It's blue for boys and pink for girls—easy!
- Starlings are great mimics. They copy many different sounds, and not just bird noises—they can do car alarms and telephones too.
- In the autumn, lots of starlings arrive from other countries to spend the winter in Britain.
- In the winter, thousands of starlings gather to roost together. These flocks perform spectacular aerobatics—a cloud of birds twisting, turning and wheeling.
- One of the reasons for the downturn in starling numbers is a shortage of nesting sites. You can help by putting up a nestbox for starlings. They need a bigger box than blue tits do, with a 45mm-diameter entrance hole.
- Take a look at 'Amazing starlings murmuration' on YouTube.

Crows

The crow family includes a number of species that you could see around your school—carrion crow, rook, jackdaw, magpie and, if you live in Ireland or north or west Scotland, the hooded crow.

Carrion crow

- This is a big black crow, and you usually see them in ones or twos. A good way to tell a carrion crow from a rook is to look at its beak. On a carrion crow, there are feathers on the top bit of the beak. You won't see these on an adult rook (although immature rooks do have them).
- Carrion crows are very clever birds. For some reason, though, they like fire, and they seem to like it too much. Sometimes they take something on fire to the nest—not a good idea.

Rook

- To tell a rook from a carrion crow, look for the pale skin at the base of a rook's beak.
- A rook is a similar size to a carrion crow. If you see lots of crows in a flock, they will probably be rooks. There might be some jackdaws in there, too.
- Rooks build stick nests high up in trees, nesting near other rooks in a rookery, but they are not good neighbours. Sometimes they steal twigs from a neighbour's nest, and sometimes they mate with another rook's partner.

Jackdaw

- Jackdaws are smaller than rooks and carrion crows. They are black with a grey patch on the back of the neck and head, and pale eyes.
- When a jackdaw calls, it goes 'jack jack'. That's why it's got 'Jack' in its name.
- Watch a jackdaw walk. It has the gait of a creature with a superior attitude!
- Jackdaws build their nests with sticks. They have been known to carry sticks more than two metres long.

Magpie

- This is a black-and-white crow with a long tail. It isn't pure black and white, though. The tail has shiny green in it and there's shiny blue in the wings.
- Five years is the typical life expectancy for a magpie, but one old bird got as far as its 21st birthday.
- Like most crows, when there's plenty of food around, magpies take more than they need and hide some so that they can come back to it later, when food is harder to find.
- Male magpies have longer tails than females.
- Magpie means 'black-and-white chatterer'. Listen to one calling and the name will make sense.
- Sometimes magpies get together with other magpies in something called a 'parliament'. This helps birds that haven't found a mate to find one. It's a bit like speed-dating.
- There are some video clips of magpies on www.arkive.org. Go to 'Birds', then 'Explore all birds', and search for 'Magpie'. Make sure you look at the right one: *Pica pica*.

Hooded crow

- Hooded crows are like grey-and-black carrion crows. They used to be thought of as the same species as the carrion crow, but in 2002 scientists decided that they were a different species.
- This is another clever bird. In the Arctic, hooded crows pull up fishing lines that have been dropped through ice-holes so that they can steal the bait from the hook.

House sparrow

Like starlings, these birds are familiar to lots of people, and sadly, also like starlings, they are not as numerous as they once were. You may well have them around your school, though.

When Jesus walked the earth, sparrows seem to have been common. Ornithological data from the first century is fairly scant, but we can guess from Jesus' comments in Matthew 10:29 and Luke 12:6 that sparrows were very familiar birds and were thought by most people to be of little value: 'Five sparrows are sold for just two pennies, but God doesn't forget a single one of them' (Luke 12:6).

Sparrow stuff

- Male and female house sparrows look different from each other. The male has a black bib and is grey on the top of his head. The female doesn't have the bib or the grey crown. The female is a duskier-looking bird, streaky on top and with a pale line running back from her eyes.
- House sparrows are cheerful chirpers—they chatter and chirp a lot.
- They pair for life, but sometimes a paired bird mates with other house sparrows. They lay two or three broods of eggs a year. Each brood normally has four eggs in it. Mum and Dad both feed the young birds in the nest but, when they leave the nest, Dad looks after them because Mum is laying eggs again.
- House sparrows are sociable birds. They often nest near other house sparrows.
- The reasons for their decline could include changes in farming that have resulted in fewer seeds for the birds to eat in the autumn and winter, a drop in insect numbers to feed the chicks of urban house sparrows, and fewer nest sites because of our well-maintained houses. The effect of sparrowhawks and cats is not easy to measure.
- You can help house sparrows by putting up nestboxes, about two metres apart. Sparrows need a box with a 32mm-diameter entrance hole.
- There are some short video clips of house sparrows on www.arkive.org. Go to 'Birds', then 'Explore all birds', and search for 'House sparrow'. Make sure you look at the right one: *Passer domesticus*.

Activities

KS1 KS2 Do the Big Schools Birdwatch

This is the schools and youth groups' part of the Big Garden Birdwatch organised by the RSPB. In 2012, over 2000 schools and nearly 90,000 people took part, and the blackbird was the commonest bird recorded. The Big Schools Birdwatch takes place in January and the counting part takes just an hour. You can do it at school or in a local park. You have to identify the birds that you see and keep a note of the highest count at any one time of each species. Birds flying over don't count.

The results go to the RSPB and help their scientists to monitor how well our birds are doing. You can register for the Birdwatch on the RSPB website (www. rspb.org.uk/schoolswatch) from the end of September. The counting takes place on a day of your choice in the second half of January. Your results can be submitted online.

To make the most of it, you will need to do some preparatory work. It's worth spending some time helping the children with basic bird identification and providing food and water for the birds in advance of the event.

KS1 KS2 Act like a bird

This is fun (for those who aren't too self-conscious) and is rooted in good observation skills. Ask the children to find and watch a bird. Then they have to act like that bird, and everyone else has to try to work out which bird it is. You could use some simple props—a piece of rolled-up newspaper to improvise a long beak or tail, for example. Put a time limit on the guessing, or it could get awkward and embarrassing if the class can't work out what bird is being acted out.

KS1 KS2 Make a bird feeder

This is a low-cost activity that can involve the whole class. Some of the feeders that you make could be hung up at school, and some could be taken home by the children. Your raw material is an empty, washed-out fruit juice carton or something similar. You need its lid too, as well as some string or wire to hang it up with.

- Use something sharp to make some drainage holes in the bottom. This will probably need to be done by an adult.
- Use scissors to make the hole on the side of the carton. Some adult help may be required. Cut three sides of a square/rectangle and bend part of the box outwards to give a bit of protection from the weather. You could make a hole on two opposite sides of the box or on just one side.
- Add the string or wire. The holes for attaching the string or wire are made with a hole punch.
- Put a handful of bird seed in the bottom and find somewhere to hang the feeder up.

You could do a bit of science with this activity. Create some different feeder designs and see which one the birds prefer, or which food types are more popular with which species.

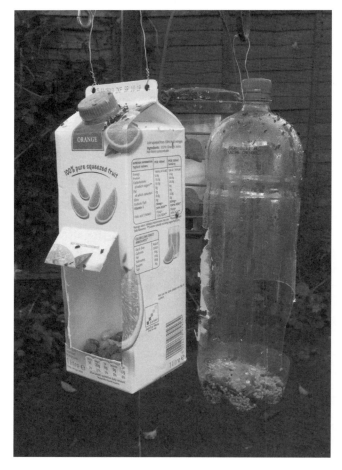

Making bird food

These two recipes are easy to make and you don't need a cooker.

Fruit and seed cake

Ingredients

- Lard
- Sunflower seeds or other bird seeds
- Dried fruit
- Peanuts—not salted ones. Buy nuts labelled as 'safe for birds'
- Mild cheese

Take the lard out of the fridge a long time before your cake-making session or it will be too hard. Grate the cheese. Cut the soft lard into small pieces and drop them into a big

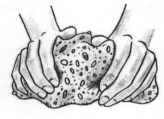

bowl. Then throw everything else in. Put your hands in and squidge them through the lard so that everything gets mixed in and sticks together.

You can give the birds their cake in clean plastic yoghurt pots or something similar. Poke a hole in the bottom of the pot and push a bit of string or wire through. Tie a big knot on the end (inside the pot), or tie it around a twig, so that the pot doesn't fall off. Push the cake mix into the pot. Stick the pot in the fridge for a while if the cake is too soft. Then hang it upside-down somewhere where the birds can find it.

You could make a log feeder for your cake. Find a log about 10cm across. (Don't use one with minibeasts living in it.) Drill some big holes in the log, then fill them with cake. You could stuff whole peanuts and sunflower seeds into smaller holes. Hang the log up.

Making bird cake is really messy. When you have finished, you'll need plenty of washing-up liquid to get the fat off your hands.

Pine cone treats

Ingredients

- Mild cheese, grated
- Sunflower seeds
- Sultanas

This is even easier to make than fruit and seed cake, and much less messy. First, find some pine cones. You need cones that have opened. Fill the gaps between the scales on the cone with the cheese, seeds and sultanas. Then tie some thread around the bottom of the cone and use this to hang the cone up.

If there is any cheese left over, spread it on the ground outside. Robins, wrens and dunnocks like cheese.

Take care with nuts

Be aware of any nut allergies in your class. You may need to exclude nuts from any of your bird feeding activities.

Reproduced with permission from *Wow! Our Amazing Planet* by David Chandler (Barnabas in Schools, 2013) www.barnabasinschools.org.uk

Make a bird table

A simple bird table is not difficult to make. You need a piece of wood about 50cm long and 30cm wide. Try to use a bit left over from something else. If you are buying new timber, check that it is FSC certified (or certified by a similar scheme), so that you know it has been responsibly produced.

Next, find some strips of wood to put around the edges, leaving gaps at the corners. The gaps will let water run off the table and make it easier to clean.

Use screws to fix the strips on. The screws go up through the main piece of wood into the bottom of the strips. (You will need to drill some holes first.)

Bang in some nails or screw in some hooks on the edge of the table, so that you can hang food or feeders from them. You don't need to use any wood preservative—it will survive for quite a while without it. Then find somewhere to put your bird table.

Place the table where you can see it, but not where cats can reach it. Keep it away from anywhere they can hide. You want to feed the birds, not the cats.

You could hang your table from the branch of a tree. Screw some eyelets into the corners of the bird table and use strong cord, wire or chains to hang it from the branch.

If there's no tree, you can put the table on a post. Bang a post into the ground so that it doesn't wobble. Then use metal brackets and screws to fix the table to the post, or use a shelf bracket to attach it to a fence post.

For an even better bird table, fix it to a movable post. It will need feet so that it stands up. You might need to peg it down as well, to stop it blowing over. If you have some plastic piping, stick it over the post to deter cats and squirrels.

Hygiene

Birds don't care about keeping their table clean, but you should. Clear up their leftovers before you put out any new food.

Try to clean the table thoroughly about once a month. Using warm water and a little mild disinfectant, give it a scrub, then throw clean warm water over to rinse it off. Let the table dry before you put any new food out.

The menu

You can buy seed to put on bird tables, but you don't have to. Birds will eat some of the food you throw away—they're not fussy. Here are some foods that you could put out for them:

- Fruit: windfall apples and pears are fine
- Bits of bread (make sure the pieces aren't too large)
- Crumbs from the children's lunchboxes: bread, cake and biscuit crumbs (but avoid crisps)
- Uncooked porridge oats
- Boiled rice (must be unsalted—birds don't like salt)
- Baked/boiled potatoes (again, unsalted)
- Raw pastry

  ## Providing water

Birds need water for drinking and bathing. Here are two easy ways you can provide some for them.

- Put some water in a clean flowerpot tray, about 20cm in diameter or bigger. Place a large stone in the tray to stop it blowing away.
- For a larger tray, use a clean dustbin lid or the lid from a redundant compost heap or water butt. Use stones or bricks to stop it wobbling, or dig a hole for it. Place some bricks or rocks in the middle of the lid.

Take care not to put your water feature in a place where cats could be a problem for visiting birds.

Keep your birdbath clean, and don't forget to change the water frequently and top it up when necessary. If it freezes over, use some hot water to melt the ice. Don't use antifreeze or salt.

(KS2) Newspaper bird sculptures

You will need newspaper, masking tape and sharp scissors.

To make your bird sculpture, choose a bird that has a very obvious feature. The shape and beak of the kingfisher help you work out what it is. The kite's tail tells you it's a kite. The long-tailed tit's tail is a big clue, too.

You can use pictures to help you make the right shapes. Once you've started, you might find that your model looks like a different bird than the one you planned, but that's OK.

Scrunch up newspaper to make the shapes. Use masking tape to hold the newspaper in place and join the shapes together. You can also use it to help you get the shapes right too: for example, wrap it round tightly to make a shape narrower.

You might be able to shape the same lump of paper into a head and body or you might need another piece of paper for the head. You can make beaks by wrapping bits of newspaper in masking tape, or, for smaller beaks, from folded layers of masking tape. If necessary, you can use sharp scissors to make the beak shape more like the real thing. (You might need to use more masking tape after you've done the cutting.)

The kite's wings get their rigidity from a strut of newspaper folded over and over, that spans the body and sticks out on each side. It sits under the front edge of the wings.

You could end up with a wonderful display of bird sculptures!

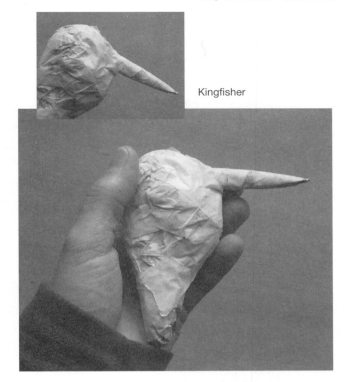

Kingfisher

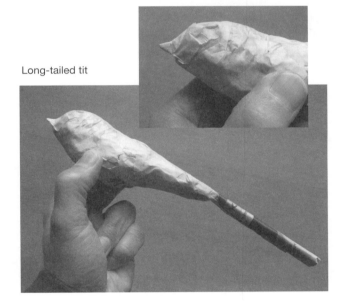

Long-tailed tit

Red Kite

Reproduced with permission from *Wow! Our Amazing Planet* by David Chandler (Barnabas in Schools, 2013) www.barnabasinschools.org.uk 23

(KS1) (KS2) ## Can you name the bird?

1. _____

2. _____

3. _____

4. _____

5. _____

6. _____

7. _____

8. _____

9. _____

10. _____

For colour images of these birds, visit the photo gallery at www.barnabasinschools.org.uk/9780857462497/

Answers on page 91

The wriggly bits

Earthworm

If you're struggling to find earthworms, find a patch of soil and dig, or have a good look in a compost heap. There are around ten different types of earthworm that live in our gardens. See if you can find these two.

Common earthworm or lob worm

- This is Britain's biggest earthworm—it can be 30cm long. It is fat, browny-purple on top and flatter at the back end. It burrows as deep as three metres beneath the surface and, if it doesn't get eaten, it can live to be very old—tens of years have been claimed.

Brandling

- Look for these smaller worms in your compost heap if you have one. Brandlings have pale yellow stripes around the body and are usually five to ten centimetres long.

Wows about worms

- Usually a worm is a boy and a girl at the same time—the technical word for it is 'hermaphrodite'. When they mate, two get together head to tail, and mating can last for hours.

- Worms don't have eyes, but their bodies detect light and they don't like it. They like to be in the dark.
- Some worms can grow a new front or back end if it gets cut off. But if you cut one in half it will probably die.
- Eating bits of dead plants might not sound very nice, but that's what worms do, and some eat soil too. They don't have teeth, but they swallow a bit of grit to help break things down. A lot of their food is sucked in, but they do bite little pieces off rotting plants.
- Have you ever wondered where the leaves on lawns disappear to? Some of them are taken underground by worms that come out at night to get a meal.
- Bits of food that worms don't digest go straight through them and come out as worm poo. Most British worms go to the loo in their tunnels, but there are two species that poo in the open, sometimes on the lawn. The posh word for their poo is 'worm casts', and they make good fertiliser.
- Worms are great for the soil. They mix it up, when they poo they add fertiliser, and their burrows let air in and help water drain through the soil. They're definitely a gardener's friend.

Worm design

Have a good look at a worm. The head end is the more pointed end. Its body is made up of lots of segments (a big worm can have 250), each with four pairs of small, stiff hairs underneath. They use these hairs for grip, to help them move. Listen carefully to a worm moving on paper. You can hear the scratching noise its hairs make.

Reproduced with permission from *Wow! Our Amazing Planet* by David Chandler (Barnabas in Schools, 2013) **www.barnabasinschools.org.uk**

Snail

Believe it or not, there are about 80 different species of land snail in Britain. Here are two common ones to look for:

Garden snail

- These are big snails. They have brown shells with dark markings.

Banded snail

- These are the stripy snails that you see. There are two species—the brown-lipped banded snail and the white-lipped banded snail. The 'lip' is around the opening of the shell next to the animal's body. It's usually brown on the brown-lipped snail and pale on the white-lipped. But… occasionally brown-lipped have pale lips and vice versa. Sometimes they don't have stripy shells, either. You could see yellow shells, brown shells, or even pink shells.

Snail snippets

- Like earthworms, snails are hermaphrodite—they are male and female at the same time.
- Some people eat snails. Garden snails are a delicacy in France.
- Song thrushes love to eat snails, too. Watch one smashing a snail against concrete or rock (its 'anvil') to break the shell. You might find an anvil with bits of broken snail shell on or around it. If you do, you'll know what happened.
- Snails and slugs move on trails of slime. If there's a snail 'racing' across a window, go inside and watch how it does it. Or try to follow a slime trail to track down the animal that left it behind.

Slug

We have about 20 species of slug in the UK. Slugs are like snails with no external shell. Most of them have a small shell hidden inside their body and a few (the shelled slugs) have a very small shell on the outside, stuck on at the back end.

One to look for is the large black slug. It's a slug, and it can be 13cm long, so it's large! But it isn't always black. There are cream-coloured ones, brown ones, grey ones and orange ones.

Slug snippets

- Shelled slugs are worm eaters. They go underground and hunt worms in their burrows.
- Look for two pairs of 'feelers' on slugs and snails. The long ones have eyes on them. They can't see very well, but they can tell light from dark. All four tentacles pick up smells, and that's how the animals find their food. Most of their 'nose' is on the short tentacles. The short ones help them taste their food, too. Try not to touch their tentacles.
- Slugs and snails have really rough tongues for breaking up their food.

26 Reproduced with permission from *Wow! Our Amazing Planet* by David Chandler (Barnabas in Schools, 2013) www.barnabasinschools.org.uk

Butterfly

There are about 60 different butterfly species in the UK. They are very closely related to moths, and we have over 2000 moth species. The main difference is that butterflies have clubs on the ends of their antennae, and most moths don't (apart from the Burnet moths, which are also brightly coloured and fly during the day). Here is a list of some of the butterflies that you might see around your school. Use a field guide to help you work out which ones you are looking at:

- Small Skipper
- Essex Skipper
- Large Skipper
- Brimstone
- Large White
- Small White
- Marbled White
- Green-veined White
- Orange-tip
- Common Blue
- Holly Blue
- Red Admiral
- Painted Lady
- Small Tortoiseshell
- Peacock
- Comma
- Speckled Wood
- Gatekeeper
- Meadow Brown
- Ringlet

Brilliant butterflies

- Butterflies smell with their antennae.
- A butterfly's mouthpart is called its proboscis. The proboscis is like a flexible straw that is used to suck up nectar from flowers. When the butterfly isn't feeding, the proboscis is coiled up.
- Butterflies are insects, so they have six legs.
- Most adult butterflies don't live very long. Some might only live for four days. Others might get as far as three weeks old. The adult Brimstone does very well—it can survive for ten months (hibernating mostly).
- To attract a female, the male's front wings make a special smell.
- A female might lay around 50 eggs. Not all the eggs become caterpillars, and not all the caterpillars will become pupae (or chrysalises). Only a few will make it all the way to adulthood.
- Butterflies survive the winter as eggs, caterpillars, pupae or adults.
- The caterpillars of many of our butterflies will eat only one or two different types of plant. These are called their foodplants.
- It's not just birds that migrate. Some butterflies do too—Painted Ladies and Red Admirals, for example.

Marbled White butterfly

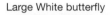

Large White butterfly

Reproduced with permission from *Wow! Our Amazing Planet* by David Chandler (Barnabas in Schools, 2013) www.barnabasinschools.org.uk

Bee

Britain is home to around 260 bee species. Most of these are solitary bees that nest in holes in the soil, brickwork or dead wood. But the bees most people know are honey bees and bumble bees—these are colonial bees.

Honey bee

- Honey bees are very important creatures. They pollinate our crops and most of our flowering plants and they make honey.
- There is an antioxidant in honey that makes your brain work better.
- A honey bee colony has a queen who lays the eggs, other females called workers, and drones (the males).
- Tree holes are good nest sites for wild honey bees, but most honey bees are kept by beekeepers. People have been keeping bees for at least 5000 years.
- Honey bees eat nectar and pollen. Honey is regurgitated nectar.
- Honey bees do the waggle dance to tell their hive-mates where to go for really good food.
- A queen bee might live to be four years old.
- Honey bee numbers have dropped dramatically. This is because of pesticides, bad weather, fewer wildflowers and the varroa mite, which is destroying honey bee colonies.
- Honey bees can beat their wings 200 times a second. That's where the buzzing sound comes from.
- Honey bees are blind to the colour red—you won't see one pollinating a red flower.
- You could check out 'Honey Bee—Teach your kids about the amazing busy buzzing insect' on YouTube. It's suitable for Foundation or Key Stage 1.

Also on YouTube, you can find:

- 'City of Bees'—a children's guide to bees (1 minute 33 seconds). The children in this video are aged about six.
- 'Sesame Street: Honeybee Hullabaloo' (1 minute 43 seconds).
- 'The Bee Movie'

You can also go to www.foe.co.uk for '20 things you need to know about bees', a free pdf download.

Bumblebee

- Most people know what a bumblebee looks like. They are bigger and hairier than other bees, and, because of this, they are out and about when the weather is cooler. There are eight types of bumblebee that are quite easy to see in this country, and another 16 that are harder to spot.
- Only the queen bumblebee survives the winter. The first signs of spring bring her out of hibernation to feed and find a new nest site.
- There may be 400 bees in a bumblebee nest.
- Don't try sniffing them, but bumblebees have stinky feet! When they have plundered most of the pollen and nectar from a flower and are on their way to the next one, their stinky feet smell stays behind. Other bumblebees smell it and give that flower a miss.
- Only the females can sting, and it's very rare that they do. You would have to be very silly or very unlucky to be stung by one of these gentle insects.
- Like honey bees, bumblebees provide us with an essential pollination service. We need bees.

- There's a new bumblebee species in town! The tree bumblebee arrived in this country in 2001. It has a black head, gingery thorax (the middle bit of its body) and black abdomen (the rear part of its body) with a white tip. It likes to nest in bird nestboxes. It does a good job of pollinating and is not thought to be a problem.
- You can help bumblebees by planting nectar- and pollen-rich flowers. Why not grow some lavender, herbs or foxgloves to help them out? There are other flowers that are good, too.
- Bumblebees can do something that other bees can't. It's called 'buzz pollination'. They use a high-frequency buzz to bring out more pollen from the flower. You might see them doing it with tomato plants.

Wasp

Everyone knows wasps and many people don't like them. But there are some good things about them.

Wasp words

- Wasps kill garden pests to feed them to their larvae. That's what they're doing early in the year when they're not seen so often. They are not a picnic problem for very long.
- Honey buzzards are not common in Britain, but they do like eating wasps—the adults, the larvae and the pupae. They raid the wasps' nest to get at them.
- Wasps make fantastic nests from spit and chewed-up wood. Some of their nests can be very large.
- Sometimes, wasps raid honey bee colonies to grab some honey. It's not a very clever move, though—the bees sting them to death.
- There can be 10,000 wasps in a single nest, but by the winter only the queens are still alive. They find somewhere to shelter for the colder months, then create a new colony when the weather warms up again.

- There are some short video clips about the common wasp on www.arkive.org. Go to 'Invertebrates (Terrestrial)', then 'Explore all terrestrial invertebrates', and search for 'Common wasp'.

Ladybird

Children love ladybirds, and they are not difficult to spot. Ladybirds are beetles and there are over 20 species in Britain.

Learn about ladybirds

- Our commonest ladybird is called the seven-spot ladybird. It has seven spots, but that doesn't mean it's seven years old. The two-spot ladybird is also very common.
- The bright colours of ladybirds are warning colours. The colours warn anything that might want to eat the ladybirds that they don't taste very good.
- If you handle a ladybird, its legs might secrete a horrible chemical on to you. It's a protective mechanism—it's not the ladybird doing a wee.
- Look out for harlequin ladybirds. These are not native to the UK and were first seen in this country in 2004. The harlequin is a big ladybird, eats food that our native species could otherwise eat, and eats other ladybird larvae. It is partly to blame for the decline of all our ladybird species apart from the seven-spot.
- Ladybirds survive the winter by hibernating. You might see a group of them tucked away in the bark of a tree, a shed, or a gap in an old window frame.

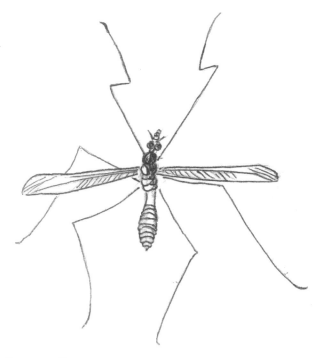

Crane-fly

Crane-fly is the posh name for the insects that most people call 'daddy-long-legs'. They are a type of fly, and, like other flies, have only one pair of wings.

Crane-fly cramming

- Crane-flies won't hurt you. They don't sting.
- Their legs come off very easily, so, if you have to handle them, be very careful.
- Their back pair of wings are not wings at all, but short, clubbed stalks called 'halteres' that help a daddy-long-legs to balance when it's flying.
- The crane-flies with pointed tails are females. The point is their egg-laying tool.
- Crane-fly larvae are called 'leatherjackets'. Starlings love to eat them. When you see a starling poking around in your lawn, that could be what it's looking for.

Spider

Spiders are not insects. They are in a group called arachnids, along with scorpions, harvestmen, mites and ticks. Like all arachnids, spiders have eight legs.

There are over 600 British spider species. Unlike insects, whose bodies have three parts (the head, the thorax and the abdomen), spiders' bodies have just two parts. The front part is called the cephalothorax. The rear part is the abdomen. The brain and the stomach are in the front bit. The heart, gut and lungs are in the back. Silk is made here, too.

Spider stuff

- You won't find a vegetarian spider—they are predators.
- Not all spiders build webs to catch their prey. Some wait patiently and ambush their dinner, and some are active hunters.
- All spiders can make at least four types of silk. The orb-web spiders (the ones that make the classic spider webs) can make five. The fifth type is what they use on the curly bits of their wonderful webs.
- Silk is made inside the spider and pulled out, not pushed out. Typically, it's the legs that do the pulling.
- Most spiders have eight eyes.
- Silk isn't used just to make webs. Spiders also use it to wrap up their victims and protect their eggs.
- Spiders have a pair of fangs that they use to paralyse their prey.
- Spiders can't eat solid food. They turn their victims to mush by vomiting digestive juices on to their catch.

Garden spider

- This is also known as the cross spider—because of the white cross on the top of the abdomen, not because of its temperament! They are big, easy to see and build wonderful orb webs.

Zebra spider

- This is a small spider with a stripy abdomen and legs. Sunny walls and sheds are good places to look for them. The zebra spider is a jumping spider. It sneaks up on its prey and leaps on it.

Woodlouse spider

- You might find one of these lurking under a log. It is a nocturnal hunter and its name tells you what it eats. It has a light-coloured, glossy abdomen and deep-red fangs. Handle with care—this one can puncture human skin.

Woodlouse

Britain is home to almost 50 different woodlouse species. A quick leg count will tell you that they are not insects—they have 14 legs. They are crustaceans, related to crabs and lobsters.

Woodlouse wonders

- To find woodlice, look under logs, rocks and rubble and in compost heaps. They have to protect themselves from drying out, so they spend lots of time in cool, damp places. They don't do much during the heat of the day. Cooler night-time conditions are much more to their liking.
- They eat bits of plants, dead or alive, and munch on rotting wood too.
- Pill woodlice roll themselves up into a ball so that they don't dry out too much. This also protects them from some of their predators. They are called pill woodlice because dodgy 'doctors' used to prescribe them as medicine.
- Woodlice wear their skeletons on the outside, so they must moult their skin if they want to grow. The rear end is moulted first, and then the front.
- Young woodlice begin their life in a pouch under the front end of their mother.

Centipede

There are about 3000 species of centipede in the world. 'Centipede' means '100 feet'—but you will never find a centipede with 100 legs because they always have an odd number of pairs of legs. (You could do some numeracy work here.)

Centipede sense

- How many legs does a centipede have? It varies—from 30 to 382.
- Centipedes are predators. That's why they move fast.
- They have venomous claws that they use to paralyse their victims.
- You can find centipedes under logs and rocks, and in the soil.
- One easy-to-see centipede is called the common lithobius. It has 30 legs. The legs get progressively longer towards the rear of the body, so when it's in a hurry it won't fall over its own feet.

Millipede

Britain is blessed with around 50 different millipede species. 'Millipede' means '1000 feet' but if you think that's how many legs a millipede has, you're wrong. Millipedes have lots of legs, but there is not a single millipede anywhere with 1000 legs.

So how do you tell a millipede from a centipede? One way is to look at the legs. A centipede has one pair per segment. A millipede has two pairs on most of its segments.

Millipede must-knows

- How many legs does a millipede have, then? You guessed—it varies. The most counted so far is 750.
- Millipedes eat bits of rotting plant, and sometimes bits of dead minibeasts. They don't need to move very fast to catch their dinner, so they don't. That's another way you can tell a millipede from a centipede.
- You can find millipedes under logs, in the soil and among fallen rotting leaves. They can push their way through the soil and leaves with quite a force. Put one in your hand and you'll feel how strong it is.
- Upset a millipede and it might release poison—but none of the ones in the UK will do you any harm.

Activities

  ### Minibeast safari

Here are some suggestions for things you can do to find and enjoy minibeasts. See page 33 for a recording chart that you can copy and use. This chart can also be downloaded from www.barnabasinschools.org.uk/9780857462497/.

- Just look! Go outside, walk along the edge of some long vegetation and just look. Children may be much better at this than adults. Their eyes are probably sharper and their shorter height makes it easier for them to spot some creatures.
- Logs and stones: Carefully lift or roll logs, stones, rocks or bricks/rubble. Take care not to squash any creatures when you put their home back in place. Release any that you have caught next to their home—let them find their own way back under.
- Compost heaps: Open compost heaps and sealed ones with lids are good places to look for minibeasts. Have a gentle rummage and see what you can find. If you don't want to put your hands in, you could use a trowel.
- White sheet: This looks very scientific! Lay a white sheet under an overhanging branch of a tree or shrub. Hold the branch and give it a sudden shake, or tap it with a stick. Just one tap should do the trick, but don't be too tentative or the creatures you want to dislodge will hold on tight. Have a good look at whatever has landed on the sheet. Afterwards, gently shake the creatures off the sheet, under the tree or bush, and let them find their own way home.

Caring for your catch

Despite their best intentions, children's fingers can squash small creatures. A good way to work with minibeasts is to equip each child (or each pair of children) with a small plastic pot and a small paintbrush. Ask them to look for minibeasts and bring the one they like best back in the pot. The brush is for handling the creatures—much better than fingers. Tell them that the one they like best might not be the one they find first.

If it's too tricky for the children to get their favourite in the pot, ask them to take you to the creature. Go through the group's catch with them. Everyone can look at everyone else's minibeasts.

Five or six children (or pairs) per group is probably enough. When you're done, ask the children to return their creatures to where they found them.

Interpreting the catch

Try to read up in advance so that you can tell the children something interesting about some of the things they have found. The facts on the previous pages will help. Use keys or identification guides to help you and the children name the creatures you don't know (see 'Further resources' on page 91). Then you can do research to find out the more interesting stuff when you are back in the classroom.

32

Minibeast recording chart

Type of minibeast	Where I found it	What I think it needs to survive	What I like most about it

Make a ladybird mask

- Photocopy the template below, or download from www.barnabasinschools.org.uk/ 9780857462497/. Use thin card to make multiple copies.
- Children should colour the mask in appropriate felt-tip colours.

- Cut out the mask shape and the eyeholes (the black circles on the template). Young children may need help with one or both of these tasks.
- Make a small hole with a pencil at either edge of the mask, near the eyeholes.
- Thread some fine elastic through the holes and knot at either end so that the mask fits comfortably around the child's head.

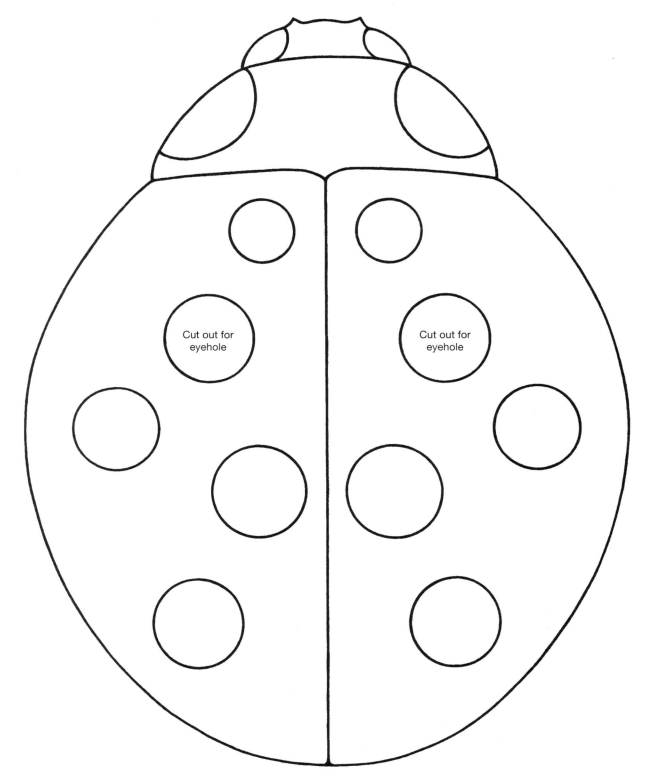

Cut out for eyehole

Cut out for eyehole

34

Make a wormery

Worm-watching is a tricky task, but a wormery makes it a lot easier. You'll need someone who is reasonably good at DIY to help you build your wormery. Essentially, it's made of two pieces of Perspex, about 30cm square (the exact size is not important) screwed on to a U-shaped wooden frame. Two extra pieces of wood are needed to make the base (see diagram below).

Add a range of soils and sand in layers. Try to find soils that are different colours so that you can see what the worms do to the soil. Then add some leaves and about ten worms. Cover the top so that the worms can't escape, and cover the sides with something opaque or keep the wormery somewhere dark.

Keep the soil damp and take a peek periodically to see what the worms have been up to. You should see that the leaves have been pulled underground and the different soil layers mixed up by the worms. You should see the worms' tunnels too. Don't keep your worms captive for too long. When you have finished, put them back where you found them.

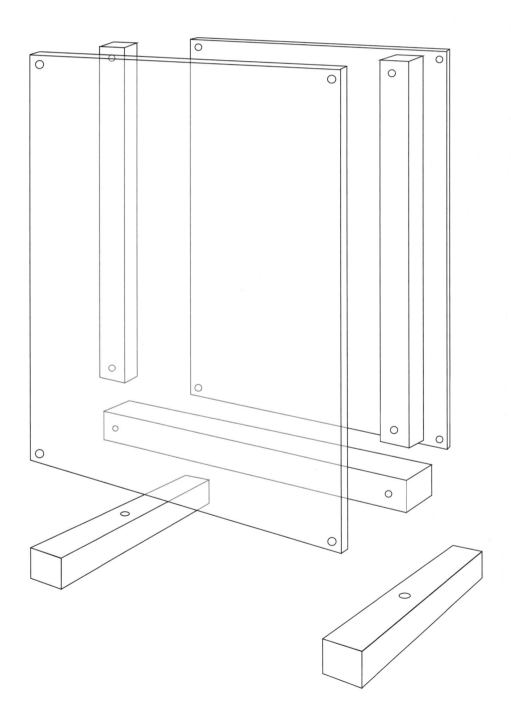

Creatures word search

Look for the names of the creatures in the word search. They may run horizontally or vertically.

```
B  U  T  T  E  R  F  L  Y  D  P  K  T  T  A
Q  T  J  K  S  B  I  R  D  I  O  P  S  W  X
G  F  D  H  R  T  M  B  G  M  O  T  H  I  O
J  O  S  S  N  A  I  L  H  R  T  S  H  Z  H
K  X  B  B  T  B  F  E  C  B  Z  W  S  W  P
F  H  F  C  G  E  O  S  L  U  G  U  E  O  I
R  T  J  S  A  E  R  W  P  G  H  T  E  R  U
O  V  U  T  H  E  D  G  E  H  O  G  K  M  R
G  R  E  H  I  P  K  Z  R  W  A  V  G  D  A
C  N  V  Y  C  T  A  A  S  P  R  F  G  N  T
```

BEE   BUTTERFLY   FOX   HEDGEHOG

SNAIL   BIRD   FROG   MOTH

SLUG   WORM   RAT

This wordsearch can also be downloaded at www.barnabasinschools.org.uk/9780857462497/

Whose world?

Creation in the Bible

The story of creation is found in the book of Genesis, which means 'beginning' or 'origin'. Genesis is the book of beginnings: it tells of the origins of the universe, the earth and its inhabitants (human and non-human). It means 'beginning', it's about beginnings, and it's right at the beginning of the Bible.

The story

Read the creation story to the children or ask the children to read it; then ask them to tell it or even act it to others. We recommend that you read it from Genesis 1:1 right through to 2:4. There are lots of different English translations of the Bible and some of them will be easier for your class to understand than others. We suggest using the New Living Translation (NLT) or the Contemporary English Version (CEV). There is a paraphrase on page 39, which would be particularly suitable for reading to Key Stage 1 children, and the story is told from the CEV on page 40. You could read it in instalments.

Creation v. evolution

There may be children who ask questions about the creation story and evolution. If that happens, it's worth explaining that there are many views among Christians on this issue. Some believe that God did make the world in six days—with a rest on the seventh. Others see no conflict between evolution and the biblical creation account. Genesis is not a scientific text and the truth is that no one knows for sure exactly how God created the universe. The book of Genesis is about the *who* of creation rather than the *how*.

Understanding the Genesis creation account

Key messages

There are three key messages to draw out from this account:

- God made the world.
- He made it very good.
- He shared the job of looking after it with humankind.

Questions for discussion with your class

Key Stage 1

- How many times does God describe his handiwork as 'good'?
- When he has finished creating the world, how does he describe it then?
- What is your favourite part of creation? What do you like about it?
- What job has he given us to do?
- What can we do to look after the world?

Key Stage 2

For Key Stage 2 you could also ask some of the following questions:

- Do you think it is important that we look after the world? Why?
- What can we do at school to help look after the world?
- What can we do at home to help look after the world?
- Is the world still good?
- Is it still as good as when it was first made?
- If it isn't, why not?
- If it isn't, do we still need to look after it?

Activities

Drawing creation

Draw a picture for each day of creation. This could be done on a big scale, with different children working on different days to produce an impressive piece of wall art.

Create a creature

Make an animal out of modelling clay. It could be a model of a real animal or something imaginary. If it's the latter, ask the makers to talk about their animal to a group or with the whole class. They can give it a name and explain how and where it lives.

Key Stage 2 extension: The garden of Eden

There is more on creation in the rest of Genesis 2. Here, you will find reference to the garden of Eden. Take a look at verse 15. This is what it says: 'The Lord God put the man in the Garden of Eden to take care of it and to look after it.'

Key message

God put man in the garden of Eden to 'take care of it and to look after it'. That's very similar to the job that humankind was given in the first chapter of Genesis.

Garden of Eden

Here's a research challenge: where was the garden of Eden? (We've included a map on page 41 that gives the answer.)

The story of creation: How to make a universe

Let's go right back to the beginning—before computers, before mobile phones, before your grandparents' grandparents' grandparents were born. That's a very, very long time ago. The truth is that no one knows exactly how long ago.

The beginning is when God made the whole universe, top to bottom and edge to edge—every little bit of it, and every big bit of it. At first there was nothing on the earth and everything was dark. But the Spirit of God was there. Then God spoke. He said, 'Let there be light.' And because he's God, there was light. God liked the light. He could see that it was good. The next thing he did was to keep the light and the darkness apart. He called the light 'day' and the darkness 'night'. That's what God did on the first day. But God didn't stop there.

The next day, God spoke again. When God speaks, things happen. So he spoke, and made the sky. The sky separated the water on the earth from the water high up in the atmosphere. That's what God did on day two. But God didn't stop there.

There were more words from God on the third day. This time he told the water on earth to gather together in one place. The water did as it was told. This made dry areas that God called 'land', and some big wet areas. God called these 'sea'. Then he took a look at his handiwork. 'Hmm. That's good,' he said.

But there was more to come. God told the earth to make lots of different types of plants, seeds for people to eat and scrummy, yummy fruit trees. The next bit was really clever. He made them so that they could go on and on and on, because they made seeds that grew into new plants just like the plants that made the seeds in the first place. The earth did as it was told and all kinds of plants were created. God took another look at his handiwork. He could see that it was good. But God didn't stop there.

God had more to say the next day, day four of his grand design. This time he spoke and made big shining lights for the sky. He knew that they would help people keep track of time—the different seasons and the years. He made two really big ones: he made the sun for the daytime, and the moon for the night time. He also made more stars than anyone can count—a number bigger than you can possibly imagine—and he scattered them across the universe like luminous confetti. Guess what God thought when he took a look at creation now? He thought it was good, of course. But God didn't stop there.

Day five was animal day. God spoke again. 'We need something for the waters. Let's have fish, fish and more fish and all sorts of other creatures, tiny ones, huge ones and everything in between. Sky, I want you to be full of birds—different coloured birds, different sized birds, different shaped birds. Let there be birds.' So that's what happened. When God looked at what he had done, he could see that it was good. Then God said, 'I want the fish to make more fish and fill the seas. And I want the birds to make more birds and fill the skies.' The world was getting busier. But God didn't stop there.

Day six was another animal day. God did more speaking and made more creatures. He made wild animals, from teeny, weeny minibeasts, so small that you need a microscope to see them, to wonderful big elephants. He made all the farm animals on day six, too. It was time for another look at his handiwork. God could see that it was good. But he didn't stop there.

'Now we'll make people,' God said. 'They will be like us. We'll let them look after all the animals.' God made men and women. Then he spoke again. 'Have children!' he told them. 'Be in charge of the earth, of all the creatures in the sea, all the creatures in the air and all the creatures on the land. There are plenty of fruit and seeds for you to eat. And there are plants for the birds and animals to eat, too.' God stepped back and took another look at everything that he had made. This time he could see that it was *very* good! Did God stop there?

Not for long, but he did have a rest the next day. And that's how God made the universe. A long time ago—even before your head teacher was born.

Reproduced with permission from *Wow! Our Amazing Planet* by David Chandler (Barnabas in Schools, 2013) www.barnabasinschools.org.uk

The story of creation (Genesis 1:1 — 2:4, CEV)

In the beginning God created the heavens and the earth. The earth was barren, with no form of life; it was under a roaring ocean covered with darkness. But the Spirit of God was moving over the water.

The first day

God said, 'I command light to shine!' And light started shining. God looked at the light and saw that it was good. He separated light from darkness and named the light 'Day' and the darkness 'Night'. Evening came and then morning—that was the first day.

The second day

God said, 'I command a dome to separate the water above it from the water below it.' And that's what happened. God made the dome and named it 'Sky'. Evening came and then morning—that was the second day.

The third day

God said, 'I command the water under the sky to come together in one place, so there will be dry ground.' And that's what happened. God named the dry ground 'Land', and he named the water 'Sea'. God looked at what he had done and saw that it was good.

God said, 'I command the earth to produce all kinds of plants, including fruit trees and grain.' And that's what happened.

The earth produced all kinds of vegetation. God looked at what he had done, and it was good. Evening came and then morning—that was the third day.

The fourth day

God said, 'I command lights to appear in the sky and to separate day from night and to show the time for seasons, special days, and years. I command them to shine on the earth.' And that's what happened. God made two powerful lights, the brighter one to rule the day and the other to rule the night. He also made the stars. Then God put these lights in the sky to shine on the earth, to rule day and night, and to separate light from darkness. God looked at what he had done, and it was good. Evening came and then morning—that was the fourth day.

The fifth day

God said, 'I command the sea to be full of living creatures, and I command birds to fly above the earth.' So God made the giant sea monsters and all the living creatures that swim in the sea. He also made every kind of bird. God looked at what he had done, and it was good. Then he gave the living creatures his blessing— he told the sea creatures to live everywhere in the sea and the birds to live everywhere on earth. Evening came and then morning—that was the fifth day.

The sixth day

God said, 'I command the earth to give life to all kinds of tame animals, wild animals and reptiles.' And that's what happened. God made every one of them. Then he looked at what he had done, and it was good.

God said, 'Now we will make humans, and they will be like us. We will let them rule the fish, the birds, and all other living creatures.'

So God created humans to be like himself; he made men and women. God gave them his blessing and said:

'Have a lot of children! Fill the earth with people and bring it under your control. Rule over the fish in the sea, the birds in the sky, and every animal on the earth.

'I have provided all kinds of fruit and grain for you to eat. And I have given the green plants as food for everything else that breathes. These will be food for animals, both wild and tame, and for birds.'

God looked at what he had done. All of it was very good! Evening came and then morning—that was the sixth day.

So the heavens and the earth and everything else were created.

The seventh day

By the seventh day God had finished his work, and so he rested. God blessed the seventh day and made it special because on that day he rested from his work.

That's how God created the heavens and the earth.

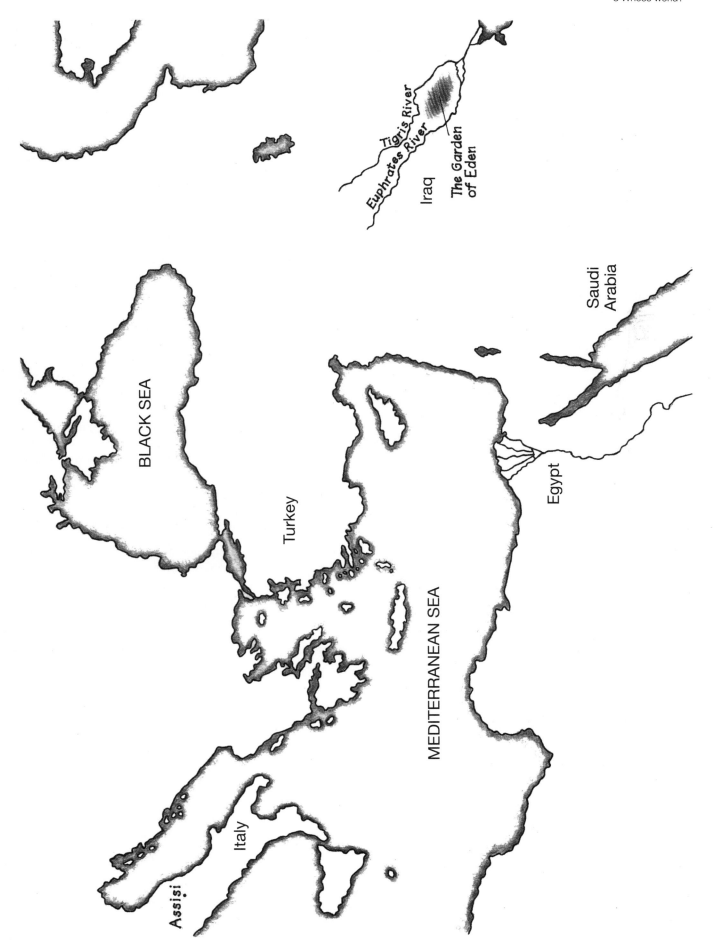

Tigris River

Euphrates River

Iraq

The Garden
of Eden

Saudi
Arabia

BLACK SEA

Turkey

Egypt

MEDITERRANEAN SEA

Italy

Assisi

Noah's ark

The story of Noah's ark is well known to many people, but don't assume that everyone in your class will be familiar with it. You will find this story in the book of Genesis, too. The biblical account of Noah's ark stretches from chapter 6:5 right through to 9:17. It's a long passage to read, so we recommend that you work with one of the versions on pages 46 and 47.

Key messages

There are two key messages to draw out from the story of Noah's ark:

- Noah's ark wasn't just about saving people. God saved animals too, and he didn't save them just because they were useful to people. Genesis 7:3 says, 'Do this so there will always be animals and birds on the earth.'
- Rainbows are a reminder of the agreement (or promise or covenant) that God made after the flood. But who was this agreement made with? Most people who know the story think that God made an agreement with humanity, but read the story closely and you'll see that the agreement is clearly bigger than that. It is also with 'every living creature' and the earth itself. The account in chapter 9 says this, or something similar, repeatedly.

Questions for discussion with your class

Key Stage 1

- How many people were on the ark? To help the children answer this one, you might need to explain that there were Noah and his wife, and his three sons and their wives. Then they just need to do some simple addition.
- How many animals were on the ark? (Answer: lots and lots and lots!)
- What sign did God give that he wouldn't destroy the earth with a flood again?
- Imagine an ark with all those animals in it. What problems might there have been?

Key Stage 2

For Key Stage 2 you could also ask:

- How did Noah find out that the floodwaters were going down? To answer this, you will need to direct the children to Genesis 8:1–13.

Activities

 ### Colouring

Colour in the Noah's ark sheet on page 43.

  ### Two by two

Most of the animals that came into the ark came in two by two. Make cards or small pieces of paper showing the names or pictures (or both) of a range of animals. There should be two cards for each type of animal. Give out the cards randomly, ask the children to memorise the animal on their card, then collect the cards in again. The children have to find their partner by moving, taking on the shape of and making the noise of the animal that was on their card. This is a good game for an end-of-term party, perhaps.

Take care with the species selection for the cards. You need to choose animals that the children know and that they can imitate. Also, don't, for example, include lions *and* tigers. There's a high chance that you will have four children roaring and no one will know who matches whom.

Here are 21 animals you could use (enough for a group of 42 children): elephant, giraffe, monkey, gorilla, snake, spider, cow, horse, sheep, pig, chicken, duck, woodpecker, butterfly, dog, cat, donkey, deer, skunk, frog, bee.

Key Stage 2 extension: Mount Ararat

Genesis 8:4 says that when the waters went down, the ark 'came to rest somewhere in the Ararat mountains'. Where are the Ararat mountains? Is there any evidence that the ark did come to rest here?

42

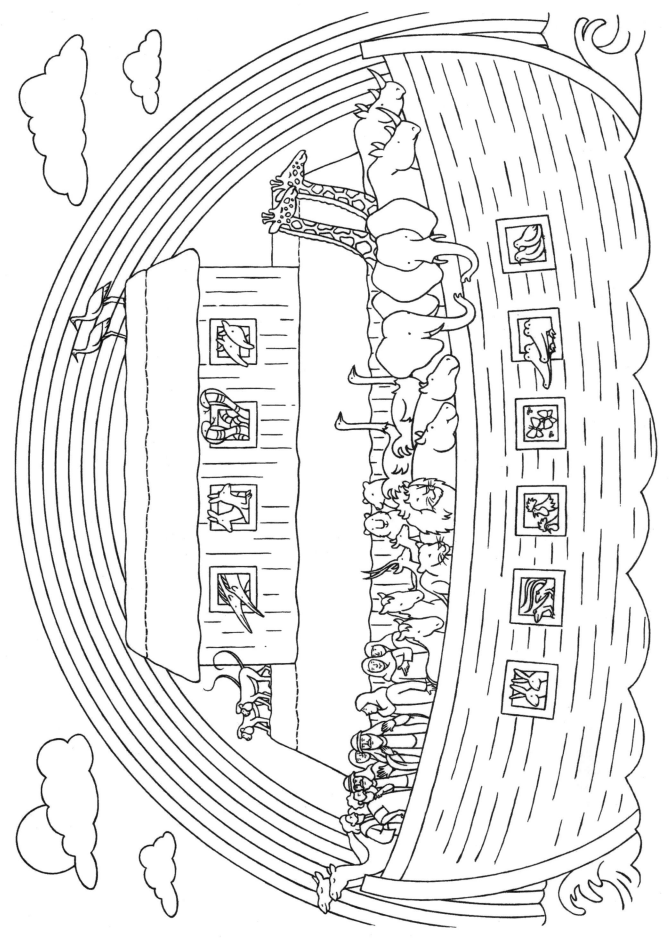

Key Stage 2 extension: Rainbows

Most people like to see a rainbow. Look at the rainbow picture in the online gallery at www.barnabasinschools. org.uk/9780857462497/. Talk to the children about how rainbows are made. Here are some notes to help you.

Sunlight is white but is made up of seven different colours—red, orange, yellow, green, blue, indigo and violet. Rainbows are made when sunlight hits raindrops and is split into its seven colours. When we see a rainbow, we see an arch of colours. A whole rainbow is actually a circle, but we can't see the bit that is below the horizon. Some lucky people have seen the whole circle, from aeroplanes.

Activities

  ### Rainbow demonstrations

- Pour water into a glass so that it is three-quarters full, and put a mirror in the glass. With the sun behind you, hold the glass so that the sun hits the mirror. Watch the wall. There should be rainbow colours somewhere.
- Let light shine through a glass prism so that you can see the colours of 'split light'. It's easiest to see the colours if you hold the prism in front of something white.
- If you have space outside, use a hosepipe to create a mist of water, and look for the rainbow colours.

  ### Rainbow collage

Use torn-up pieces of magazine paper to make a big rainbow collage on a wall.

  ### Rainbow memory

Create a mnemonic to help the class remember the colours of the rainbow.

  ### Rainbow animals

As a class, create a huge rainbow. Then stick lots of pictures of colourful animals on it to remind everyone of the promise that God made to every living creature. The children could draw and paint the animals them-selves, cut them out from magazines or use the templates provided on page 45 (also downloadable in a larger format, for easy colouring, from www. barnabasinschools.org.uk/9780857462497/).

These include some wonderfully colourful animals:

- Keel-billed toucan: an exotic bird that lives in Central and South America.
- Mandarin: a stunning duck, originally from eastern Asia. Mandarins have escaped from captivity and now live in the wild in this country.
- Mandrill: an African monkey with a colourful face and a colourful bottom.
- Milk snake: this animal has some great stripes. It is not dangerous but it looks like other snakes that are, which gives it some protection. Sadly, the stripes also lead people to kill it because they think it is dangerous. The milk snake lives in the Americas.
- Poison dart frog: lots of different types of frog are in this group of Central and South American amphibians. Not all of them are colourful but most of them are. Their bright colours tell predators that they are not for eating. Native Americans have used chemicals from a few types of poison dart frog as poison for blowdarts.
- Clownfish: the film *Finding Nemo* made these fish famous. There are about 30 species of clownfish. They swim in the Pacific Ocean, the Indian Ocean and the Red Sea.
- Leichhardts grasshopper: a fantastic grasshopper that lives in northern Australia.
- Red Admiral: a handsome butterfly that you could see in your garden or around the school grounds.

To help you colour in these animals, we have included photos of them in the online gallery. You can find this at www.barnabasinschools.org.uk/9780857462497/.

44 **www.barnabasinschools.org.uk**

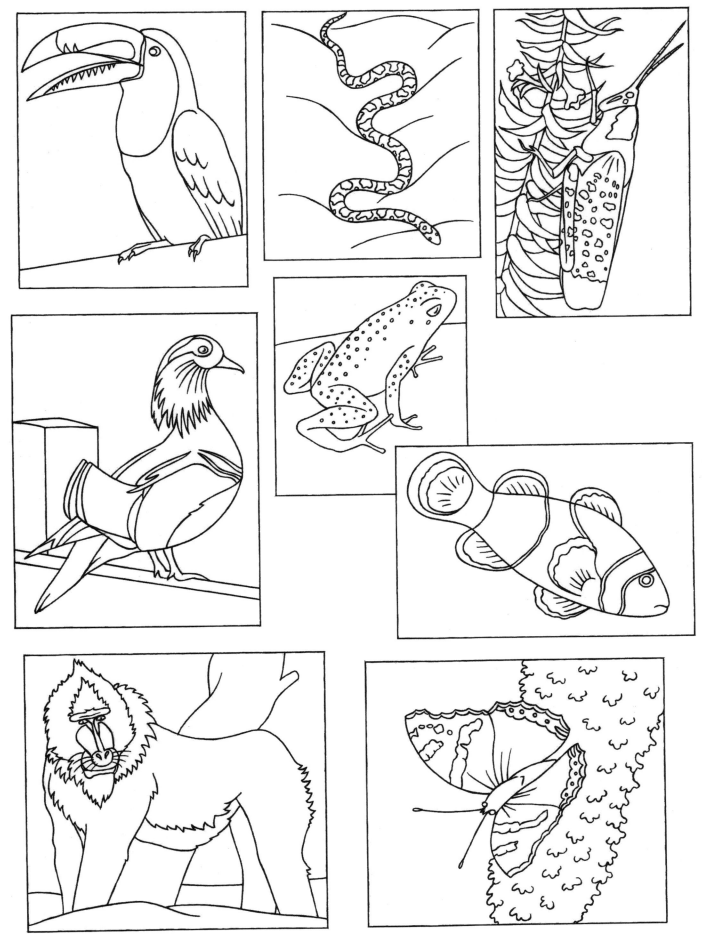

The story of Noah's ark

Noah builds a boat

Adam and Eve had many children. These children grew up, got married, and had many more children. Before long the earth was full of people.

But almost all of the people were very bad. They hurt each other a lot. All they could think about was how to do bad things.

God was very sad. He didn't want all the evil to go on. So God decided to flood the whole earth.

Noah loved God. He was the only good man in the whole world. God didn't want Noah and his family to get punished. They would need protection from the big flood.

'Noah,' said God, 'build a huge boat!' 'OK, Lord,' said Noah.

Noah and his family worked and worked. They chopped down trees. They made boards. They put the boards together.

Once the boat took shape, they covered it with tar so the water couldn't get in. The boat was called an ark.

Finally, when Noah and his family finished the ark, Noah's family and many, many animals would fit inside. The ark was huge!

The big flood

It took a long time for Noah and his family to finish the ark. But finally they did.

'It's going to rain soon,' God said. 'Now gather two of every kind of animal. Take them all with you on the ark.'

Noah gathered the animals just as God said. Then he and his family went into the ark, and God shut the door.

The rain started to pour down.

It rained hard and long. Puddles turned into lakes. Everywhere the earth started to flood. But Noah's ark floated! The water rose higher and higher. After forty days and nights, everything everywhere was under water.

Then the rain stopped.

Everyone in the whole world drowned except the people and animals on the ark.

It took a long time for the water to go down. So Noah and his family waited. The ark came to rest on top of a mountain. As soon as the water dried up, Noah opened the door. People and animals ran out.

'Thank you, God!' said Noah.

God was happy to hear Noah's praise. He promised never to flood the earth again. He set a rainbow in the sky to remind people of his promise.

'Never again will I destroy the earth like that,' God said. And God always keeps his promises.

FROM *THE EAGER READER BIBLE* (CANDLE BOOKS, 1998)

The zoo that floated

It all happened a long time ago. Noah took up boat-building. He built a big boat, and a lot of people thought it was a very strange thing to do. In those days, there were some horrible things going on in the world. There were very few good people. God had made all those people and he wasn't happy about the way they were behaving. It made him sad. He decided that there needed to be a fresh start, and to do that, he decided to flood the earth.

Now Noah was one of the very few good people. He lived a good life and obeyed God. God spoke to Noah and told him his plans, and he told him to build a boat. But he didn't just say, 'Build a boat, Noah.' He told him how big it should be, that it should be three storeys high and that it should have a door on one side.

God promised Noah that he would keep Noah and his family safe—Noah and Mrs Noah, their sons, Shem, Ham, and Japheth, and their wives. God told Noah to bring a male and a female of every kind of animal, bird and reptile on to the boat. God wanted to keep them safe too. Noah did what God said, even though people laughed at him. They couldn't work out why he was building a huge boat.

It took a long time to build that boat. Finally, the day came when God said to Noah, 'Take your family on to the boat, and take all the animals too. I want you to do this so that there will still be animals and birds on the earth. It's going to start raining in a week, and it won't stop for 40 days.'

Noah was 600 years old when he walked aboard his big boat. He finally got everyone in. All his running, wriggling, flying, hopping, squawking, roaring (and, to be honest, some of them a bit smelly) passengers were on board. But there was a problem. Who was going to shut the door? If they couldn't shut the door, the boat would sink. Someone had to do it. So God helped out: he shut the door.

It started to rain. Water came up out of the ground, lots and lots of it, and down out of the sky, even more lots of it. It rained and rained and rained. Noah had never seen so much water. No one had. They certainly wouldn't go thirsty!

The water got so deep that the mountain tops were covered in it. All that was left alive were Noah, his family and his unusual list of passengers.

It was five whole months before the water started to go down. Imagine sharing a boat with all those animals for all those months. Imagine the noise. Imagine the smell. The water went down bit by bit. Eventually, Noah's big boat came to rest in some mountains.

Noah wanted to know if they could get off the boat yet, so he let a raven go, but it just kept flying around and had to come back again. So he tried the same thing with a dove. The dove also came back to the boat because it couldn't find anywhere to land.

A week later, Noah tried sending the dove again. The dove came back with a leaf in its beak. That meant the water must be at least low enough for the trees to be sticking out above the surface.

A week later, he let the dove go for the third time—and he never saw it again. Noah made a hole in the roof and took a good look around. He could see that the water had almost gone.

It was a bit longer before the earth had dried up properly. Then everyone left the big boat, including all the smelly passengers. Everyone was pleased to get out of the floating zoo.

After all this, God made a promise: 'I promise every living creature that the earth and those living on it will never again be destroyed by a flood. And I've put a rainbow in the sky to remind you of the promise that I have made. When I see a rainbow, I will remember my promise.'

St Francis

Despite what the Bible says, the church and Christians have not always done a very good job of looking after creation. Thankfully things are improving and the church is beginning to get the message. Christians who care about creation are not a recent phenomenon, however. Witness St Francis…

Read the story to your class (see page 49). As an alternative, this is a great story for some of the children to act out for the rest of the class or in an assembly, or to tell to others.

The prayer of St Francis of Assisi

This is a very famous prayer. In fact, though, we can't be sure that St Francis wrote it. There is no record of it before 1912.

Lord, make me an instrument of your peace.
Where there is hatred, let me sow love;
where there is injury, pardon;
where there is doubt, faith;
where there is despair, hope;
where there is darkness, light;
and where there is sadness, joy.

O Divine Master, grant that I may not so much seek
to be consoled as to console;
to be understood as to understand;
to be loved as to love.
For it is in giving that we receive;
it is in pardoning that we are pardoned;
and it is in dying that we are born to eternal life.
Amen

Key message

One key message to draw out from the story of St Francis is that it is not only in modern times that people have cared about creation.

Activities

Where is Assisi?

Use the map on page 41 to show the children where Assisi is. Alternatively, see the Key Stage 2 extension below.

Creation favourites

Find out more about your favourite part of creation—a plant, animal or landscape—and tell the rest of the class about it.

Key Stage 2 extension

Ask the children to find out where Assisi is. When they have done this, ask them to find out the names of some of the birds and flowers that St Francis might have seen. Then they can make a guess at which ones might have been his favourites, and why.

The story of St Francis

Over 800 years ago, in 1181 or 1182, a baby boy was born. No one knew it at the time, but this was a child that people would be talking and writing about hundreds of years later. The boy was Italian and his dad gave him the name Francesco. We know him as Francis (which is the English version of Francesco), or St Francis, to be precise.

Francis lived in a very rich family and went to lots of parties—his father had made a lot of money by selling cloth—but in 1205 things changed. Francis was a soldier now and was sent to war. Then he had a vision from God that changed his life. He came home to Assisi wanting to do everything he could to help poor people. He spent his time looking after people with leprosy, a horrible skin disease.

Francis loved animals too and called them his brothers and sisters. There are lots of stories about Francis and animals. Some people must have thought he was a bit strange.

Maybe you have heard a vicar giving a sermon at church. Francis gave sermons to wild birds! One story about him tells how he was on a journey when he noticed some trees with lots of birds in the branches. He made his friends wait while he went to preach to the birds. Francis told the birds that they should love God and praise him. He told them that God had given them feathers and wings and everything else that they needed, that they were noble and had 'a home in the purity of the air', and that God looked after them.

The birds didn't fly away: they gathered around Francis. One of his friends said that the birds let Francis touch them as he blessed them. After this, Francis felt bad that he hadn't told the birds about God before, so he told all sorts of animals to love and praise God.

All those years ago, Francis taught that God had made a good, beautiful world that needed some loving care because of the wrong things that people had done. He believed that it was humankind's job to look after nature.

Francis died when he was in his 40s, on 3 October 1226. One story says that just before he died, he thanked his donkey, and the donkey cried. Two years later, the Pope made Francis a saint. 4 October is still a day when many churches remember St Francis. On the nearest Sunday to this date, they bless animals at a special church service.

Reproduced with permission from *Wow! Our Amazing Planet* by David Chandler (Barnabas in Schools, 2013) www.barnabasinschools.org.uk 49

St Dave?

In the Catholic Church, people become saints by canonisation, but that is not the case across the whole of the Christian Church. In some of the New Testament letters in the Bible, the word 'saints' is used in a way that suggests that it refers to all believers. God still talks to people today, and there are still Christians who are passionate about caring for creation. Dave Bookless is one of them. This is his story. (He agreed that we could call him St Dave as long as we included a question mark!)

Read Dave's story to your class, using one of the versions on pages 51 and 52.

Key messages

There are two key messages to draw out of Dave's story:

- God still speaks to people about how he feels about his world and how we should look after it.
- There are people who are doing something about it.

Dave and his children

Dave and Anne have four daughters aged between 10 and 17.

They all think the G-Wiz car is cool.

Their youngest daughter uses the energy monitor to see what household appliances are using the most electricity. Then she nags everyone if they are using those things.

Their eldest daughter likes to buy clothes in charity shops. Reusing clothes is an easy way to do something positive for the environment.

One of their daughters is a vegetarian. Eating less meat is good for the environment, but there are plenty of people who care about creation who are not vegetarians.

We asked Dave what children could do to care for creation. This is what he said:

- Walk to school if you can.
- Use the car less. Encourage your family to walk, cycle or take the bus.
- Don't throw rubbish on the ground.
- Recycle everything you can.

- Try to eat food that has been produced in this country—the nearer to home the better.
- Grow something you can eat, even if it is only in a plant pot or window box.
- Learn about ten birds that you can see where you live. Feed the birds.
- Get an energy monitor at home.

Activities

  Dave Bookless question time

Ask your class these questions after they have read or listened to Dave's story:

- Which country was Dave born in? (India. For KS2 you could also ask for the city. The answer is Calcutta.)
- Name the two countries where Dave went to school. (India and England)
- What did Dave play marbles with in India? (Beetles that rolled themselves into balls)
- Why did Dave put oil in the inkwells? (To try to fit in)
- What was Dave's job before he was a vicar? (He was a teacher)
- What did God say to Dave when he went to throw away the rubbish? (How do you think I feel about what you are doing to my world?)
- Name two things that Dave and his family have done to look after God's world. (Didn't use disposable nappies; grow their own food; walk or use their bikes; bought an electric car; have never flown in an aeroplane to go on holiday)

Find out more about the story of A Rocha UK by visiting their website: www.arocha.org/gb-en.

(KS1) Dave's story

This is a true story about Dave. Dave is older than your parents but younger than your grandparents. He was born in a big city in India. His parents were teachers at a Christian college.

As a child, Dave was full of mischief. He loved riding his bike and exploring. When he was 7, he rode on the back of a scooter to a lake where he saw storks, herons, kingfishers and egrets. He thought they were brilliant.

Dave went to a boarding school in the mountains, but he wasn't always happy. He was lonely and missed his home, but he did enjoy walking in the school grounds. He saw golden orioles and other beautiful birds and did lots of drawings of wildlife. He played marbles with beetles that rolled themselves into balls (please don't try this!). It went wrong if a beetle unrolled itself.

When he was 10, the family moved to England and Dave went to a new school. Dave looked English but spoke with an Indian accent. Imagine that! He watched TV and heard pop music for the first time. He found it hard to make friends. To try to fit in, he did something naughty. In those days, children wrote with pens that they had to fill with ink. The ink was kept in inkwells, which were like little buckets of ink in the desks. Dave put oil in the inkwells and then the pens stopped working. He was in big trouble and had to do extra tests as punishment—but he did really well in those tests!

Dave's school had its own bird reserve with ducks and geese that had to be fed. Dave fed the birds and this got him interested in caring for wildlife. Some of the ducks were very rare and they bred. When this happened, a children's TV programme about wildlife was made at the school. Dave was getting really interested in birds. Today, Dave says, 'They are colourful; they sing and are always there wherever you live. You never know what you are going to see.'

When he was 13, Dave went to a Christian summer camp and became a Christian. That changed his life. He loved to visit the river and woodland near his school, where there were kingfishers, dippers and owls, and he started a school birdwatching club.

When he grew up, Dave became a teacher. Then he became a vicar in London. He was on holiday, staying on an island, when God spoke to him. He needed to get rid of some rubbish, but there were no rubbish collections. Someone who lived there told him to throw it into the sea. 'How do you think I feel about what you are doing to my world?' said God. Dave says it wasn't a voice you could hear, but the words hadn't come from inside Dave.

Since then, Dave and his family have changed the way they live to help look after God's world.

- They decided not to use nappies that you throw away. That's good because the used nappies end up buried in the ground and stay there for a very long time.
- They grow their own food.
- They walk or use their bikes as much as they can. Their four daughters liked walking to school because it meant they got more time with Mum or Dad.
- They have an electric car that does not pollute the air.
- The family nearly always avoids flying in aeroplanes to go on holiday.

Dave isn't a full-time vicar any more. He works for A Rocha, a Christian conservation organisation, and is studying again. He is learning even more about what the Bible says about looking after creation. Dave and his wife Anne started A Rocha UK. They found a piece of land that had dumped cars and lots of rubbish on it and helped to turn it into a country park. Now it is a good place for people and wildlife.

God still talks to people, and there are still Christians who care about God's world.

Dave's story

This is a true story about Dave. Dave is probably older than your parents, but younger than your grandparents. He was born in Calcutta, a very big city in India. His parents were teachers at a Christian college.

As a child, Dave was full of mischief. He loved riding his bike and exploring. When he was 7, he had a lift on the back of a scooter to a lake near Bangalore. There he saw lots of birds and thought the storks, herons, kingfishers and egrets were brilliant.

Dave went to a boarding school in the mountains in India, in a place called Ooty, but he wasn't always happy there. He was very lonely and got homesick. The school was set in very large grounds and he did enjoy going for long walks there. He saw golden orioles and other beautiful birds and did lots of drawings of the wildlife. He played marbles using beetles that rolled themselves up into balls (please don't try this!). Sometimes things went wrong when a beetle unrolled itself.

Three years later, the family moved to England. This was a very difficult time for Dave. He looked English but spoke with an Indian accent. Dave was 10 now—and watched TV and heard pop music for the first time. He found it hard to make friends in his new school. In those days, children wrote with fountain pens that they filled with ink from inkwells. (An inkwell is like a little bucket of ink built into the desk.) To try to fit in, Dave got up to mischief: one day, he put oil in the inkwells, which made the pens jam up. This was the day before the school tests started. He was in big trouble and had to do extra tests as his punishment—but he did really well in those tests!

The school that Dave went to is probably very different from your school. It had its own bird reserve with ducks and geese that had to be fed. Dave was one of the boys who fed the birds and this got him interested in caring for wildlife. Some of the ducks were very rare ducks and they bred. When this happened, a children's TV programme about wildlife was made at the school. Dave was getting really interested in birds. Today, Dave says, 'They are colourful; they sing and are always there wherever you live. You never know what you are going to see.'

When he was 13, Dave went to a Christian summer camp and became a Christian. That changed his life. He was happier at school now and loved to visit the river and woodland where there were kingfishers, dippers and owls. He also started a school birdwatching club.

When he grew up, Dave became a teacher: he taught RE, Art, History and Geography. Then he became a vicar of a church on the edge of London. He was on holiday on an island off Cornwall when God spoke to him. Before coming home, they had to get rid of their rubbish, but there were no rubbish collections. One of the people who lived there told Dave to throw it off a cliff into the sea. 'How do you think I feel about what you are doing to my world?' said God. Dave says it wasn't a voice you could hear, but the words hadn't come from inside Dave. It certainly got Dave thinking.

Since then, Dave and his family have made lots of changes to the way they live so that they can do their bit to help look after God's world. Here are some of the things they have done:

- They decided not to use disposable nappies. That's good because disposable nappies end up buried in the ground and stay there for a very long time.
- They started growing their own food on an allotment.
- They walk or use their bikes as much as they can. Their four daughters liked walking to school because it meant they got more time with Mum or Dad.
- They changed their car to a G-Wiz, an electric car that does not pollute the air.
- The family nearly always avoids flying in aeroplanes to go on holiday.

Dave isn't a full-time vicar any more. He works for A Rocha, a Christian conservation organisation, and is studying again—learning more about what the Bible says about looking after creation. Dave and his wife Anne started A Rocha UK. Its first big project was helping to turn a piece of land that had dumped cars and lots of rubbish on it into a country park. Now it's a good place for people and wildlife.

God still talks to people, and there are still Christians who care about the natural world.

Whose fault?

God gave humanity the job of looking after his world on his behalf, but our track record on this front hasn't always been very impressive. The Christian message, though, is one of hope—hope for humanity and hope for everything else in creation, too. This section could be a discouraging one, but sections 5 and 6 will redress the balance.

This section provides information that illustrates the poor job we have done. It talks about threatened species, places and climate change. Choose the stories that you think will work best with your class.

Troubled species

Polar bear

Everyone knows what a polar bear looks like. It is the white bear of the Arctic, the world's biggest bear. It can weigh up to 600kg. You could work out how many children it would take to match that weight.

If you are thinking about polar bears with your class, ask them whether the Arctic is around the North Pole or the South Pole (it's the North Pole) and what the region that surrounds the South Pole is called (the Antarctic). Ask them to imagine living in a place where the winter is permanently dark and the summer is permanently light. In the very far north, the sun goes down in October and stays down until February is almost over. And it can be 50°C below freezing. Imagine that!

Typically, polar bears are active all year round. They have been created for an Arctic existence, with 10cm of fat, topped off with black skin and a dense fur coat. Their ears and tail are small, which helps to reduce heat loss. They are great swimmers, using their front feet as paddles and their back legs to steer. When food is hard to find, this Arctic predator can slow down its metabolic rate to save energy. This is called 'walking hibernation'.

Blizzards are an occupational hazard of life in the Arctic. When they come, a polar bear will dig a shallow snow den and hunker down. The snow that covers the bear provides extra insulation during its time in the den, which can stretch to several days. Sleeping is high on the list of a polar bear's favourite things. So are ringed seals.

We might think polar bears look cuddly, but the ringed seal knows that they are not. Ringed seals are this beautiful bear's main prey. The seals swim under the sea ice, but, being mammals, they have to come to the surface sooner or later to breathe. They do this at breathing holes that they make in the ice, sticking their heads above the surface about four times an hour.

Polar bears know that the seals do this, and they can smell the breathing holes, even when they are buried beneath a metre of snow, from over half a mile away. They have a very good sense of smell and their eyes work very well too. To get their next meal, this superb predator waits at a breathing hole. In any one area there will be a number of breathing holes, and a seal could pop up at any of them. If the bear chooses the wrong breathing hole, it has to wait a bit longer to eat. If the seal chooses the right breathing hole, it gets to live a bit longer. Polar bear hunts fail more often than they succeed: less than one in 50 brings in a seal dinner.

Canada is home to more than 50 per cent of the world's 20,000–25,000 polar bears. The big problem for polar bears is climate change. As the climate warms, the sea ice melts. Within half a century, Arctic summers could be devoid of sea ice. There is less ice now than there used to be, and, as there is a limit to the length of time that a polar bear can swim, some have drowned. Less ice also makes it harder for polar bears to find food.

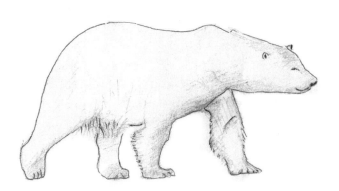

Blue whale

The blue whale is the biggest creature alive today. To put things in perspective, a big blue whale is nearly 34 metres long, can weigh 200 tonnes, has a heart that is as heavy as a car and a tongue that is as heavy as an elephant, is the biggest mammal ever, and is a similar size to a very big dinosaur (although dinosaurs were reptiles, not mammals).

This remarkable mammal can be found in most of the world's oceans. It is not just birds that migrate: other animals do, too, including the blue whale, which seeks out warmer waters in which to spend the winter. The blue whale is a baleen whale: it has baleen plates instead of teeth. Baleen works like a giant tea strainer, filtering this leviathan's food from the ocean waters. Its diet is not what you might expect for such a huge animal. Blue whales eat krill—crustaceans that are about 5cm long. What these animals lack in bulk, the whale makes up for in the quantity it eats. It has a daily krill intake that totals four tonnes or more.

A blue whale can stay under water for 50 minutes and reach a depth of 500 metres, where its thick blubber helps to keep it warm. When it comes to the surface and blows, the pillar of spray can be almost nine metres high. This animal is said to be the noisiest in the world: its underwater singing can be heard by other blue whales as far as 1600 kilometres (1000 miles) away. Ask the class if they could sing a song that could be heard that far away!

Blue whales breed when they are somewhere between five and ten years old, breeding once every two or three years. You would expect the world's biggest creature to produce a big baby, and, after being pregnant for ten to twelve months, they do. A baby blue whale tips the scales at around 2.7 tonnes and is about eight metres long. The calves are fed on their mother's nutritious milk for a year. There is some impressive weight gain, with the calf growing by over 90kg a day during its first year in the ocean. A blue whale can live to be 90 years old.

Commercial whaling almost wiped out the blue whale. They were hunted for their blubber, which was turned into oil. In 1931, whalers killed almost 30,000 blue whales. Shipping causes problems for blue whales, too: when a big ship collides with a big whale, it can kill the whale. By the 1960s only a few hundred remained and in 1966 hunting blue whales was banned. About half a century ago, this fantastic creature was almost one for the history books, but their numbers have increased and in 2007 the world population was estimated at 4,500 individuals. This is definite progress, but the world's blue whale population is still just a small fraction of what it once was.

Dodo

Mauritius is an Indian Ocean island, east of Madagascar, and was the home of an iconic bird—the dodo. In Portuguese, 'dodo' is a bit of an insult. It's a bit like calling someone a simpleton. The name reflects the attitude that Portuguese sailors had to this bird, a bird that had no fear of people and readily approached the newcomers to the island. The sailors arrived in 1598 and found a bird that was new to science. By 1690, less than 100 years later, it had been wiped out.

Dodos were large, round, grey birds and are thought to have weighed 20–23kg. No bird of this weight can fly, and the fearless, inquisitive dodo was easy to club to death, making an easy meal for the hungry sailors. The newcomers brought pigs and monkeys to the island, and these caused problems too, dining out on the chicks and eggs of Mauritius's dodos.

Kemp's Ridley sea turtle

Like snakes and lizards, turtles are reptiles. There are seven species of sea turtle in the world, and Kemp's Ridley is the one that is most at risk: the global population could be as small as 1000 individuals.

This is not a big sea turtle. The biggest is the Leatherback, which can weigh 680kg and be over 1.8m long. Kemp's Ridley is the smallest sea turtle, with a big one measuring just 70cm long and weighing around 60kg. It has a parrot-like beak which it uses to munch its way though crabs and other invertebrates. It is a species of the Atlantic Ocean, and is particularly fond of the Gulf of Mexico: the only known nesting areas are in Texas and Mexico.

Whereas some sea turtles use the cover of darkness to lay their eggs on a beach, Kemp's Ridley's strategy is one of en-masse daytime egg-laying. Females breed when they are 10–15 years old and can lay eggs up to three times in one season, with each clutch containing 90–130 eggs. A female intent on egg-laying will swim hundreds of miles to get to the right beach, and may well return to the beach where she herself found her way out of an egg. Turtles use a tailor-made egg-cutting tooth to get out of the egg. This is called a 'caruncle'. Once the turtle is out of the egg, it heads straight for the ocean.

Fifty or sixty years ago, this species was almost extinct. People had been collecting their eggs and had been taking many more than the turtle population could cope with. Turtles were accidentally trapped in fishing nets, too, and coyotes (a type of wild dog) added to their woes by raiding their nests.

Things have improved for these fascinating reptiles, but they are not in the clear yet. Their nesting areas are protected now, and fishing nets have been made less hazardous by the addition of 'turtle excluders', but the population is not getting much larger.

There are five short video clips of this species on www.arkive.org. Go to 'Reptiles', then 'Explore all reptiles', and search for 'Kemp's ridley turtle'.

- The female digging the nest and preparing the egg chamber (44 seconds)
- The female laying eggs (50 seconds)
- The female going back to the sea (25 seconds)
- The hatchlings coming out of the nest (30 seconds)
- The hatchlings heading for the sea (34 seconds)

Natterjack toad

The blue whale may be the noisiest animal in the world, but the natterjack toad is the loudest amphibian in Europe. It can't compete with the blue whale, but, when a male calls, the sound can be picked up over two kilometres away. Natterjacks are found from Spain and Portugal to the Baltic countries, Belarus and the Ukraine. They live in the UK, too, but are not very common here. If you see one, look for the narrow yellow stripe that runs down the centre of its back. A big natterjack can be about ten centimetres long, though seven or eight centimetres is a more typical length.

Perhaps surprisingly, natterjacks are not very good at swimming. If they are in deep water and are unable to haul themselves out on to land, they may drown. They can jump, but not very far. If you disturb one, it will probably jump and then run rather than hop or walk.

Natterjacks are good at climbing up banks and can dig burrows. They are mostly active at night, and may use a burrow to provide protection from the heat of the day. Sometimes they use burrows made by other animals. They hibernate in burrows, too—which they may make themselves, or 'borrow' from other species, including rabbits and sometimes sand martins.

Heaths and sand dunes with shallow ponds are good natterjack habitats. Males call to attract a female—though some don't bother, relying on the calls of their neighbours instead. The females lay their eggs in a string that contains 1500 to 7500 eggs and can be two metres long. A lot of heathland has been lost and we also have less sand dune habitat. This, together with the drying out of ponds, has been a problem for the natterjack toad in most of its European range.

In Britain, natterjack toads are protected by law. There are fewer than 50 breeding areas, but many of these are on nature reserves and a species action plan has been written to help conserve natterjacks. Their presence in some areas is the result of reintroduction programmes, which has brought this noisy amphibian back to places that had lost their original natterjack population.

There are some short video clips of natterjack toads on www.arkive.org. Go to 'Amphibians', then 'Explore all amphibians', and search for 'Natterjack toad'.

- Overview (33 seconds)
- Locomotion (25 seconds)
- Reproduction (59 seconds)

European eel

This is a fish that looks like a snake and has a truly remarkable lifecycle. European eels lay their eggs near the Bahamas, in a part of the Atlantic Ocean called the Sargasso Sea. The leaf-like larvae that emerge from the eggs move towards northern Europe, carried along by the North Atlantic Drift (a warm sea current). The larvae are in no hurry and it might be two years before they get near Europe. They eat plankton along the way and, as their destination gets closer, they turn into 'glass eels': these are transparent and about seven centimetres long.

The glass eels move from the saline sea into European rivers, changing form again when they enter fresh water. They turn into elvers, and are now more recognisable as small eels. The elvers swim upstream and change into yellow eels, with browny-yellow bellies. Elvers will negotiate seemingly impassable obstacles in their quest to get upstream. They will even climb up rocks and waterfalls.

It can take up to 20 years before an eel is ready to breed. The mature eel—the silver eel—has a white belly, silver flanks and big eyes. The females are larger than the males and can be a metre long. A male is around 40cm in length. It is the silver eels that tackle the return journey across the Atlantic to the Sargasso Sea, where they spawn and then die.

The European eel copes with life in fresh water, sea water, flowing water and still water. It is a very feisty creature and will even leave the water and move over land when necessary. Since the 1970s their numbers have plummeted by around 95 per cent. Human beings are implicated in this massive decline—through overfishing, building dams for hydroelectric schemes that even eels can't get over, and our contribution to climate change, which is affecting the North Atlantic drift. A parasite has added to the eel's woes.

Jellied eels are a famous East London delicacy. The advice now is not to eat any eels until things have improved for this snaky fish.

Go to www.sustainableeelgroup.com to see 'The eel story' (an animation), play 'Ely the Eel' and see a short video on eels from Autumn Watch.

Giant clam

Molluscs include cockles, mussels, snails, slugs, squids and octopuses. There are somewhere around 100,000 different species alive today and the giant clam is the heaviest one of them all. Big ones can be over a metre across and weigh 300kg. Giant clams live on tropical reefs and most are found in the Pacific Ocean. This mega-invertebrate has two interlocking heavyweight shells, with wave-like lips. Look between the lips and you'll see its soft, fleshy 'mantle'. The mantle is green, yellow or yellowy brown, with 'windows'—clear or pale spots that light can shine through.

Giant clams get their food in two ways. Much of it comes via a special arrangement with algae that live in its mantle. The algae find safe haven by living in the clam, and can get the sunlight that they need to photosynthesise. They pay their way by making proteins and sugars—excellent sustenance for a giant clam. The clam does fend for itself to some degree. It siphons water in and out of its mantle—one hole for incoming water, another for outgoing water. It's a filter feeder, extracting plankton from the water flow, with gills positioned underneath the siphon.

The clam's 'output' siphon is also used for reproduction. Eggs and sperm are jettisoned into the sea, both from one clam, along with plenty of water. Young clams enjoy a week or so of aquatic mobility before settling down. And the place where they settle is where they spend the rest of their days—which, for a giant clam, could add up to over 100 years.

You may have heard stories of giant clams trapping and swallowing divers. These tales are not true—there is nothing to fear from this oversized mollusc. The truth is that its shells close at a speed that is very unlikely to trap any diver.

It's a great beast, but its future is not entirely secure. Clam meat (the muscle that closes the shell) is, according to some, a delicacy. The demand for their meat, and for clams to live in aquaria, has seen their numbers fall. There are no longer any giant clams around Fiji. On a more positive note, farming giant clams has provided some respite for those living in the wild, and giant clams have been reintroduced around Tonga.

There are some short giant clam videoclips on www.arkive.org. Go to 'Invertebrates (Marine)', then 'Explore all marine invertebrates', and search for 'Giant clam'.

- Overview (44 seconds)
- Giant clams spawning (36 seconds)

Atlantic cod

Not many people have seen a live wild cod. This big sea fish is a favourite for eating: cod and chips is one of the original British takeaways. The Atlantic cod has a big head for its body size, with a 'whisker' at the front of its lower jaw. Some are pale grey, while those that live in water where there are algae are greenish or reddish.

Atlantic cod lay their eggs between January and April. One fish can lay as many as five million eggs. It takes between a fortnight and a month for the eggs to hatch. A cod's growth is fuelled by a diet of swimming crabs, small marine invertebrates and little fish. Some varieties of cod mature quicker than others: three years can be all it takes for a coastal cod, whereas the migratory cod takes between eight and twelve years to reach maturity. A wild cod can live to be 13 years old or older. A big migratory cod weighs eight kilograms.

The cod's popularity as a fish to eat has led to its downfall. Too many were taken out of the sea for food, and the stock of cod was being depleted faster than it could replenish itself. In 2001, cod fishing in the North Sea was banned, so we hope that cod numbers will recover. They are still fished sustainably around Iceland, where the catch rate is such that the population is able to maintain its numbers.

Their tasty, flaky, white flesh is a product that people enjoy. Cod liver oil is one that, on the whole, we don't enjoy so much, but it is still put to good use. It's not to everyone's taste, but it is loaded with vitamins A and D.

Dormouse

The hazel dormouse is one of our cutest mammals and, along with bats and hedgehogs, one of a select group that hibernate. Unlike mice, it has a long, furry tail. Its eyes are big and beady, well suited to its nocturnal lifestyle. A dormouse measures 6–9cm, plus an extra 5.5–8cm for the tail, and tips the scales at somewhere between 15g and 30g.

Dormice are found in deciduous woods, coppiced woodland and hedgerows. Most of the time, they stay out of sight in nests made of bark and grass, a metre or so from the ground. But when the sun goes down, the dormice go up. This is a creature of the treetops, heading up high to feast on nuts, fruits, flowers and insects.

Dormice spend a lot of time sleeping and can hibernate for seven months, from October to April. The similarity of their name to *dormir*, the French verb for 'to sleep', is probably not a coincidence. When the time comes to hunker down for the colder months, a dormouse builds a leafy nest near or just below the ground. During hibernation, this attractive rodent rolls into a ball, slows down its metabolism and draws on the fat reserves that it built up in the autumn by scoffing hazelnuts, to help it survive. Dormice do come out of hibernation every now and then to feed on food stores that were cached in advance.

Breeding takes place once or twice a year, with pregnancy lasting 22–24 days (compare that with the blue whale's long pregnancy). Each litter contains between two and seven young dormice. Some dormouse families are raised in holes in trees or special nesting boxes. A dormouse can live to be five years old.

In the UK, dormice are found in Wales and Southern England, but their numbers have gone down because of habitat loss and habitat fragmentation. Dormice are not keen to cross the gaps that separate areas of suitable habitat.

Reproduced with permission from *Wow! Our Amazing Planet* by David Chandler (Barnabas in Schools, 2013) **www.barnabasinschools.org.uk**

Horrid ground weaver

Around 35,000 species of spider have been identified, and this could be one of the rarest. You might imagine that it lives in an obscure tropical forest or a far-flung desert, but it doesn't. It lives near Plymouth in Devon. It's not a big beast: it's a 2.5mm-long money spider. It was 1989 before we even knew it existed. After that, nobody saw one again until 1995, and that's the last anyone has seen of it. A grand total of nine have been recorded—ever. The horrid ground weaver is known from just two limestone quarries, one of which is an industrial estate now.

'Buglife' is the organisation that is trying to save this little gem. Something needs to be done to help, but it's a difficult job. The horrid ground weaver is not big or easy to spot and, to make it even more of a challenge, its favourite places seem to be cracks, nooks and crannies in the rock, and it's active in the dark. A 'bug hoover' is one tool that is being used to try to find some.

Juniper

Saving species is not just about animals. The juniper is a plant that is native to the UK, and it is struggling. Of Britain's native conifers, only three are evergreen—the yew, the Scots pine and the juniper. Larch is a native conifer too, but not all conifers are evergreen. The larch isn't: it sheds its needle-like leaves every autumn.

Unlike some conifers, the juniper grows very slowly. Its leaves are blue-green needles, which make a juniper bush a well-protected place for birds to nest, as well as an important habitat for insects, lichens and fungi. The leaves may be prickly but rabbits and red deer still feed on them.

Some juniper trees are male and some are female. There are cones on male and female trees. The small yellow male cones drop off after releasing their pollen. The female cones look like berries. When they are ripe, they are purple, but at first they're green and can take as much as three years to acquire their waxy, dark purple finish. The ripe cones, or juniper berries, are gobbled up by hungry birds, who play their part by transporting the seeds and depositing them elsewhere, in their droppings. People seek out juniper berries, too—for cooking and, most famously, to add flavour to gin.

Today, only about 400 hectares (a big international football pitch is about 0.8 hectare) of juniper survive in the wild in Britain, their numbers having been reduced by a root-killing fungus and by the challenges of a changing climate. There is a Biodiversity Action Plan for the juniper—an official plan that aims to give the juniper a brighter future. The Chilterns are one of Britain's juniper hotspots. Here, A Rocha works with Natural England (the government's conservation body) to make a better future for this spiky bush. This work includes planting young juniper trees, so their numbers are going up.

Activities

  ### 'Why save species?' discussion

Key message

God gave mankind the job of looking after creation. Remember what it says in Genesis 1 and 2? But we haven't always done this very well.

Pitched appropriately, this discussion can work with Key Stage 1 or Key Stage 2 students.

Ask your class why they think it is important to save species. This is not a simple question and the level at which it is explored will depend on the group you are working with. Here are some reasons that you can weave into your discussion:

- Every species needs other species, whether it's for food, for somewhere to live, or for help in dispersing its seeds. If one species disappears, it could have a bad effect on other species.
- We need other species to survive. The meat, fruit and vegetables that we eat may be farmed now, but they all came originally from wild species. We still eat species taken straight from the wild: if you like fish, think about where it comes from (some is farmed, of course). Three species of grass—wheat, rice and corn—provide the main food for people all over the world.
- We need other species to survive. People have used plants as medicine for thousands of years. The Navajo Indians used almost 200 different plant species to make people better. Some of our modern medicines are based on compounds found in plants. Over 1500 years ago, the Chinese were treating malaria with sweet wormwood *Artemisia annua* leaves. Western medicine uses this plant to make artemisinin, a very effective treatment for malaria that is recommended by the World Health Organisation.
- We need other species to survive. Think of the building materials the natural world provides— wood, reeds and straw, for example. Think of the insects that pollinate fruit trees and other plants. Think of the species that help to clean up water. Think of the species that help to look after the climate. Think of the species that help to make soil. Think of the plants that make oxygen: where would you be without that?
- Wildlife and wild places give a lot of people a lot of pleasure. Wildlife is good for you.

For a Christian there are other reasons to save species. In a letter that the apostle Paul wrote to Christians in Rome, he said, 'God's eternal power and character cannot be seen. But from the beginning of creation, God has shown what these are like by all he has made' (Romans 1:20).

Paul is saying that creation tells us about God. For the Christian, that has to be a good reason to look after it.

There's another reason, too. Remember what it says in Genesis, right back at the beginning? God told people to look after creation. For the Christian, if God tells us to do it, we should do it. It's the first commandment.

 ### Writing about struggling species

Write a story or poem to tell the story of a species that is struggling to survive. Write it from the point of view of the animal or plant.

You could ask the children to read their stories or poems to the rest of the group. Ask them how the writing made them feel.

  ### True or false?

This activity can be done inside or outdoors and can be more or less active, as you choose. It's a good way to reinforce earlier learning.

You read out some statements about the species and the children have to decide whether each statement is true or false. If it's true, they run to the 'true' corner (if you have space to run). If it's false, they run to the 'false' corner. Alternatively, you could nominate people to be 'true' and 'false' and ask the children to run to them. Once you've discussed the answer, the children return to the middle of the space and another statement is read out. If you're doing this activity in the classroom, you could ask the children simply to put their hands up if they think the statement is true.

On page 60 are some statements about each species. Use the ones that you think will work with your group. You could make up some of your own, too.

Polar bear

- The polar bear is the world's biggest bear. *(True)*
- Polar bears live in the Antarctic. *(False: they live in the Arctic)*
- Ringed seals are a polar bear's favourite food. *(True)*
- Polar bears wait at ice holes to catch ringed seals, but they don't usually manage to catch one. *(True: fewer than 1 in 50 attempts are successful)*
- Hunting for fur coats is the main threat to polar bears. *(False: climate change and melting sea ice is the main problem)*

Blue whale

- The blue whale is the biggest animal alive today. *(True)*
- A blue whale's tongue is as heavy as five elephants. *(False: it's as heavy as one elephant)*
- Blue whales have sharp teeth. *(False: they have baleen plates that filter krill from the water)*
- A blue whale can hear another blue whale from 160 kilometres away. *(False: it's 1600 kilometres away)*
- A baby blue whale weighs almost three tonnes. *(True: 2.7 tonnes)*
- Blue whales were hunted for their blubber. *(True)*

Dodo

- Dodos were very good at flying. *(False: they couldn't fly)*
- Dodos are very rare now, but you can still see them at London Zoo. *(False: they have been extinct since 1690 at the latest)*
- Portuguese sailors ate lots of dodos. *(True)*

Kemp's Ridley sea turtle

- Kemp's Ridley sea turtle is the biggest sea turtle in the world. *(False: it's the smallest)*
- Kemp's Ridley sea turtles eat lots of crabs. *(True)*
- There are fewer Kemp's Ridley sea turtles than there used to be because people took too many of their eggs and the turtles got tangled up in fishing nets. *(True)*

Natterjack toad

- Natterjack toads have a green stripe down their back. *(False: it's yellow)*
- Natterjack toads don't swim very well. *(True)*
- Natterjack toads hibernate in burrows. *(True)*
- Natterjack toads lay their eggs in a long string. *(True)*

European eel

- European eels lay their eggs near Cornwall. *(False: they lay their eggs in the Sargasso Sea, near the Bahamas)*
- The European eel is a fish that can move over land and climb up rocks and waterfalls. *(True)*
- A European eel can be 20 years old before it breeds. *(True)*
- To help the European eel, you should eat them as often as you can. *(False: please don't eat them until things have improved for the eel)*

Giant clam

- The giant clam is the heaviest mollusc in the world. *(True: a big one can weigh about 300kg)*
- Algae attach themselves to the giant clam. *(True: in return, the algae get a safe place to live and the sunlight that they need to make food)*
- A single giant clam is male and female at the same time. *(True: if you want to use the scientific word for it, they are 'hermaphrodite')*

Atlantic cod

- There are fewer cod than there used to be because too many have been caught for people to eat. *(True)*
- Cod fishing around Iceland doesn't make their numbers go down. *(True: the fishing methods used there are sustainable)*
- Cod liver oil contains vitamins C and E. *(False: it contains vitamins A and D)*

Dormouse

- Dormice hibernate in winter. *(True: sometimes for seven months)*
- Dormice are most active on hot, sunny days. *(False: they are nocturnal)*
- Dormice live in woods and hedgerows. *(True)*
- Dormouse numbers have gone down because people keep waking them up and they are not getting enough sleep. *(False: the loss of woods and hedgerows, and the breaking up of their habitat into smaller bits, are the problem)*

Juniper

- The juniper is a conifer. *(True)*
- The juniper loses its leaves in the autumn. *(False: it's an evergreen)*
- When they are ripe, juniper berries are bright red. *(False: they are dark purple)*
- A Rocha is helping to plant young junipers in the Chilterns. *(True)*

Troubled places

The sea

What lies beneath the sea is, for most of us, an invisible world. More of our planet is made up of sea than land, and the vast majority of the species that live in the sea are still unnamed. We know so little of the riches and beauty of the marine environment, but we are destroying it before we have even discovered what lives there.

The ocean is the Lord's because he made it. (Psalm 95:5)

But what about the ocean so big and wide? It is alive with creatures, large and small. (Psalm 104:25)

Close to home

Stunning marine environments are not just found in distant tropical waters. There is beauty beneath the seas surrounding the UK, too, but we haven't been looking after our seas very well. Overfishing has depleted fish stocks, oil and chemical spills pollute the water, rubbish is dumped in the sea, and poorly sited windfarms cause problems for wildlife.

We are home to millions of breeding seabirds, including the Manx shearwater and the Northern gannet. Almost the entire world population of Manx shearwaters breeds here, then spends the winter off South America. This remarkable migrant depends on us. Most of the planet's Northern gannets breed here. This spectacular plunge-diver depends on us, too.

Thousands and thousands of species live in the UK's seas. Corals build coral reefs (yes, there are coral reefs around the UK), and huge basking sharks filter the sea for food. There are starfish and sunfish, jellyfish and anemones, killer whales, seals and dolphins. The sea provides oxygen to help us breathe and it limits climate change by soaking up greenhouse gases. We need to look after it.

Did you know that the baked bean sea squirt and the fried egg sea anemone can both be found in the sea around the UK? But their names don't mean that you can eat them.

Lundy

Head west out to sea from Ilfracombe in North Devon and eventually you'll get to Lundy, a granite island five kilometres long and no more than 750 metres wide. Fewer than 30 people live there, but plenty of people take a day trip to visit the island. The island and the seas that surround it are a very special place for wildlife. Eight types of coral are found there, as well as lobsters, grey seals and much more. And there is nowhere else in the world you can see the Lundy Cabbage, a rare plant that looks nothing like the cabbages you buy at the greengrocers.

The name 'Lundy' comes from the old Norse word for 'puffin'. Sadly, by 2005 only two or three pairs of puffins were breeding on Lundy. Their decline seemed to be due to two man-made problems: we had fished too many sand eels, one of the puffin's favourite food items, and black rats were plundering their eggs and chicks. Black rats found their way on to the island from shipwrecks a long time ago, and have also wreaked havoc with the Manx shearwaters breeding on Lundy. Conservationists decided to get rid of the rats. This took two years but it seemed to work. With time, we hope, the seabird numbers will increase again.

The waters around Lundy became a voluntary marine nature reserve back in 1971. Fifteen years later, the area became England's sole statutory Marine Nature Reserve, and in 2010 this chunk of sea, where the Bristol Channel merges into the Atlantic Ocean, was designated as a Marine Conservation Zone. To protect this precious area, different zones have been set up for different activities— sailing, fishing and diving, for example. A 'no-take zone' has been set up—over three square kilometres of sea where no one is allowed to take any plant or animal. This had never been done in this country before, and seems to have brought some good results. There are more lobsters and they are bigger than before.

This will probably help people who catch lobsters to eat, too. The thinking is that once the lobsters have grown up, some of them will leave the no-take zone and take up residence in areas where they can be legally caught. It could be good news for lobsters and good news for people.

More on coral reefs

A coral is a simple animal, related to jellyfish and sea anemones. Its body is essentially a tube with a hole at one end only. Unlike vertebrates, which wear their skeletons on the inside, invertebrate corals make a stony skeleton on the outside of their bodies. Sea anemones don't do this. The coral's stony skeleton protects and supports the animal that lives inside it. A coral reef is a mass of corals living in close proximity. It is hard and stony, and is thought to be one of the planet's richest wildlife habitats.

Most coral reefs are found in the Pacific and Indian Oceans, around south-east Asia and in the Red Sea. At 2000 kilometres long, Australia's Great Barrier Reef is the biggest and most famous of them all.

Despite their diversity and beauty, the world is losing its coral reefs. Greenhouse gases are part of the problem. The world's seas have been soaking up CO_2, which makes them more acidic. This makes it harder for corals to make their stony exoskeletons, and the water also dissolves the coral. The sea is warming and corals are very sensitive to water temperature: when things get too warm, the corals evict algae. The algae feed the corals and give them their colour, so, when the seas warm up, the corals bleach and often die. Pollution increases nitrogen levels around reefs—and algae flourish. In fact, they flourish too well, stopping light from getting through to the coral. Rubbish can do the same thing, and traps reef wildlife. Coastal development causes erosion, which means more sediment around reefs. This too blocks out the light.

Sometimes the damage is more direct. It's hard to believe, but tourism infrastructure has been built on coral reefs! Cyanide is used to stun fish, but it kills corals. Explosives are used to catch fish, but they destroy parts of the reef. Coral reefs are used to provide building materials. Careless tourism can cause problems, too: anchors damage reefs, and people take coral souvenirs.

One in four of the world's sea-living species are found on coral reefs, although, of course, there are plenty of species that we haven't discovered yet. Given that coral reefs account for less than a thousandth of the world's oceans, their species richness is all the more remarkable. Here is some information about some of these species.

Clownfish

This is the fish made famous by the film *Finding Nemo*. Clownfish come in different colours but most of them are orange with white stripes. They live in the Indian Ocean, the Pacific Ocean and the Red Sea. Look for them where there are sea anemones. Clownfish grab their food among sea anemone tentacles. Those tentacles can sting, which makes it tricky for other fish to grab the clownfish.

Green turtle

This is one of the world's biggest sea turtles and can weigh 300kg. Its shell is broad and smooth, and it is an excellent swimmer. But we have caused problems for green turtles. Discarded plastic bags can look a lot like jellyfish. The turtle eats the bag, thinking it's a jellyfish, and dies as a result. Some green turtles get tangled up in fishing nets, some are killed by boat propellers, and people steal their eggs.

Sea anemones

Our oceans are home to over 1000 species of sea anemone. These relatives of corals are so called because of a resemblance to the flower that bears the same name. The biggest ones can measure a staggering 1.8m from side to side. Some have hundreds of tentacles. These tentacles are venom-packed, so all an anemone has to do is sit and wait for an unsuspecting fish to come a bit too close.

Sea snakes

Yes, there are snakes that live in the sea. They are related to cobras and are very poisonous. The beaded sea snake packs the most lethal punch. Just three drops of its venom can kill eight people. On a more positive note, you are very unlikely to be bitten, and their fangs are short.

Sea snakes spend most of their time in the sea and can remain submerged for an hour before coming to the surface to grab some air. They have a flattened rear end to increase their swimming speed, and, to keep the water out of their nose, can cover their nostrils with special flaps. A typical sea snake is around two metres long. These beautiful creatures are killed for food and for their skin.

Parrotfish

Here's an interesting fish. Its main food is algae and, to reach it, a parrotfish tears lumps of coral off the reef where the algae live. Parrotfish get their name from their teeth, which are joined together to make a tool that looks like the beak of a parrot. It's the right tool for the job: the teeth grind the coral up so that the hungry fish can get at the algae. As a byproduct of this process, lots of small bits of coral come out of the other end of the fish, and these make up a large proportion of the sand wherever you find parrotfish. They are a very common fish in tropical coral reefs all over the world.

Around 80 species of parrotfish have been named, with the biggest being about 120cm long. A parrotfish doesn't stay the same colour for ever: it changes its pattern and colour through its life, and some are able to switch from one colour to another very quickly. That's not the only thing they can change. They can also change their gender. A group of parrotfish will be made up of a few females and a lone, dominant male. The biggest or feistiest female will not only take on his role should he disappear, but will take on his gender too.

Sea sponges

No one knows how many types of sea sponge there are, but the scientists' best guess is somewhere around 10,000. They are animals but they are animals with chlorophyll, the pigment that we associate with plants. In fact, until the late 1800s, they were regarded as both animal and plant. A single sea sponge is male and female. It can do the female's job during one breeding attempt and become a male the next time.

Sea sponges stay still, placing themselves where the food will come to them. Some sea sponges fix themselves on to something—a rock, for example. Others are freestanding and can grow much larger, even big enough for someone to stand in. To survive, they draw in water and take their food and oxygen out of it. The water that comes out brings waste products and carbon dioxide with it.

Animals that don't move need a way of defending themselves against would-be predators. Sea sponges do this by covering themselves with toxins and sending toxins into the nearby water, too.

Sea sponges could provide us with drugs that will help people with cancer, malaria and tuberculosis. Some antiviral drugs are made with sea sponge compounds.

Activities

Coral drama

Use the information that we have provided, with some additional research if necessary, to write a short play about life on a coral reef. Make costumes or puppets, and props or a set, and perform your coral reef drama. Try to include a few amazing coral reef facts and a simple conservation message. You could use other class members as an audience, or children from another class. You could even perform your masterpiece in a school assembly.

Clownfish research

Find out more about clownfish and then watch part of *Finding Nemo*. If it's the end of term, or for a special treat, you could even watch the whole film.

Beachcombing

If you have ready access to a beach, or are planning a trip to one, spend some time beachcombing. The children will need clear instructions and good supervision because not everything on our beaches is suitable for children to handle. There's a learning point in that, though. Ask the questions, 'Where did this item come from? What should have happened to it?'

Look especially for empty shells and rubbish. If the rubbish is safe to handle, see if you can work out where it came from: if it's labelled packaging, that will give you a clue. Think about the creatures that lived in the empty shells. Try to identify them and find out about their lifestyle.

If you are not able to do this as a school activity, you could encourage the children to try it during the school holidays, with appropriate parental support.

Fish and chips

Be a fish detective. Find out where the fish in the fish-and-chip shop or the supermarket came from. The Marine Conservation Society's Good Fish Guide provides information about responsible fish eating. You can find it at www.goodfishguide.co.uk. As an extension activity, why not have a fish-and-chip meal?

Woods and forests

Close to home: temperate deciduous woodland

Woods can be great places for wildlife, great places to play and great places to find some respite from the hectic pace of modern life.

A temperate deciduous woodland is a wood of deciduous trees in a temperate region. A temperate climate is one without extremes of hot or cold. Deciduous trees shed their leaves in the autumn, lie dormant over the winter, then wake up again and grow a new set of leaves in the spring. There was a time when Britain was covered in woodland, and most land in this country, if left alone, would turn back into woodland over time.

Today, however, most of our woodland has gone. We have cleared it away to make space for farming, used the wood for fuel without allowing it to regrow, and built houses, factories, roads and offices on the land. Only about ten per cent of Britain's woodland has survived.

There are four main tree species to look for in a British wood—the mighty, wrinkly-barked oak, the black-budded ash, the towering, smooth-barked beech, and the more delicate, papery-barked birch. Different woods have different characters.

Beech trees block out the light. The sunlight struggles to reach the ground, so few plants can grow there. A beech wood can be a shady place—a good retreat in the heat of the summer.

Where oaks are the dominant species, the wood has a very different feel. Oaks let much more sunlight through and the woodland floor can be alive with violets, bluebells and primroses. An oak wood can be a very biodiverse place (a place with a great variety of plants and animals). It would take an expert to identify them, but there are almost 200 different species of moss and lichen that make their living in oak woods—on branches and trunks and at ground level.

As a rule of thumb, the first three centuries of an oak tree's life are the time when it grows. It spends the next three centuries not doing much, and the next three gradually fading. Oak trees can live to be over 1000 years old, and there are plenty that are thought to have been alive since before England came into existence as a united country, in AD927. They are great for wildlife: over 400 invertebrate species have been found on oak trees.

When the light can get into a wood, smaller trees and shrubs gain a foothold and fill the space—hawthorn, holly, hazel and rhododendron, for example. Grasses and ferns form the next layer down, and beneath them, given enough light, fungi, ivy, mosses and lichens find their place. Rotting leaves and wood bring more diversity to this wonderful habitat. Lift or roll a log carefully and you could find beetles, woodlice, spiders, centipedes and millipedes.

Ancient woods

Where a wood is believed to have been around since at least 1600 (or 1750 if it's in Scotland), it's called an ancient wood. Woods that are this old have a good chance of being natural rather than planted woodland. It's possible that some ancient woodland has a much longer history and may date back 10,000 years—to the days of the wildwood, just after the last ice age. About 20 per cent of our woods are ancient. These are home to more threatened species than anywhere else in this country. It's very important that we look after them well.

Working with woods

Woods are a wonderful renewable resource that, if managed well, can be harvested again and again. We used to do this more than we do now. There was a time when people made their homes in woods, and their cows and pigs grazed there. Woods were coppiced or pollarded. These techniques allowed the wood to be harvested in a way that was sustainable: people cut it, left it alone, and more would grow. Most of our native trees regrow after they have been chopped down. Woods provided fuel for burning, as well as building materials for houses, fencing, furniture and even battleships.

A coppiced tree is cut down close to ground level. New shoots grow from the stump and can be harvested as poles some years later. Then the stump grows more poles, which can be cut again and again. A coppiced woodland may be managed on a rotation, cutting different areas in different years. A freshly coppiced area lets in lots of sunlight and brings the colour of spring flowers into the woodland.

Pollarding is simply coppicing done higher up the tree. This technique was used to protect the new growth from grazing animals. The trees were cut somewhere between 2.5 and 4 metres up, so when the stump was shooting, the shoots were too high for the animals to reach but could still be harvested when the time came.

If you go for a woodland walk, look for coppiced and pollarded trees. In many woods, coppicing or pollarding stopped a long time ago, but you can still spot the trees that have been coppiced or pollarded. You may see pollarded willows on riverbanks, too. These old woodland management methods are good for wildlife as well as people and are now used by some organisations to improve woods for biodiversity.

Do we like rhododendrons?

They may look stunning, but rhododendrons are not meant to be here. Their natural home is the Himalayas, and it was over-enthusiastic Victorian plant collectors who introduced them to the UK. Rhododendron is not good wildlife habitat, is highly invasive, kills off the plants that are meant to be there and is very hard to get rid of. Conservationists put a lot of effort into eradicating it—in Snowdonia, for example, and at Burnham Beeches in Buckinghamshire. It's a difficult job because if a small piece of root is left in the ground, it will grow. Good stewardship is not necessarily about leaving things alone, especially when we caused the problem in the first place.

Struggling woodland birds: willow tit and lesser spotted woodpecker

The willow tit looks a lot like the marsh tit: in fact, it was the late 1800s before ornithologists worked out that they were two separate species. It's a tit with pale cheeks, a black bib and a black cap. Its numbers have crashed by about 90 per cent since the 1970s, and scientists estimate that there are only about 8500 pairs left in this country. They have completely disappeared from some areas. Because of the drop in numbers, it now has the dubious honour of being on the Red List of birds of conservation concern.

Willow tits breed in a range of woodlands, but they like damp conditions. Conservationists are trying to discover what has gone wrong for the willow tit. It could be that other tits out-compete them, that our woods are no longer of the right quality, or that great spotted woodpeckers are eating them.

Two black-and-white woodpeckers can be seen in this country. The common one, the one that comes to quite a few bird feeders, is the great spotted woodpecker. Lesser spotted woodpeckers are smaller (about the size of a sparrow) and much harder to see. If a birdwatcher sees one of these, it's been a good day.

The lesser spotted woodpecker is hard to see because it's small and searches for its invertebrate food at the tops of trees, where it can be hard to pick out. In this country, most of them are in south-east England. In the 1970s there were four times as many as there are today. The scientists think that we now have just 1400–2900 pairs.

Scientists are trying to find out what's gone wrong here, too, so that action can be taken to improve the lot of this charming woodpecker. Deer could be the problem: there are more of them than there used to be, and they might be making it harder for the woodpeckers to find bark beetles, one of their favourite food items.

Activities

  ## Make a woodland journey stick

First, find your woodland. When you get there, each child will need a reasonably stout stick, about 30–45cm long, and enough wool or string to wrap round the stick. Tie one end of the wool/string firmly to one end of the stick. As you walk, the children should collect natural items to remind them of their journey—a leaf, a twig, a moulted feather and so on—and bind each item to the stick by wrapping the string or wool around it. Attach the items in order as you find them. When you have finished, the stick is a visual reminder of the journey, with natural artefacts that connect with different stages of the route.

Don't pull the sticks from something living: pick them up off the ground. Avoid sticks that have a living creature on them, and remind the children not to attach anything that's still alive to their journey stick.

  ## Tree identification

Visit a wood and identify the main trees that are growing there. There are leaf and winter twig ID charts on the Woodland Trust's Nature Detectives website (www. naturedetectives.org.uk). These are free to download, and there are lots of other free downloads here, too. When you have identified the trees, find out more about them. What do their seeds look like? How do they disperse their seeds? Which animals eat their seeds or other parts of the tree? An older group of children may be able to tackle more types of tree.

  ## Bark rubbings and leaf prints

Use these old stalwarts to help your class remember what the trees you identify look like. Oak, ash, beech and birch are good to start with.

  ## Tree planting

Planting trees or a hedge is something very practical that you could do to make a difference. It's an activity that most children will really enjoy and, for some, the experience of handling a spade and getting a bit muddy may be completely new. With the right instruction, suitably sized spades and appropriate supervision, this is something that Key Stage 1 children can manage.

You may be able to get a free pack of trees to plant from the Woodland Trust: take a look at www.woodlandtrust. org.uk. If you buy your own trees, plant them between October and March. If you do that, you can work with bare-rooted trees, which are not very expensive.

 ## Winnie the Pooh

Younger children especially might like to listen to some Winnie the Pooh stories, which are set in the Hundred Acre Wood. You could link this activity to your literacy work.

 ## How high?

This is a fun way to estimate the height of a tree. Walk away from the tree until, when bending over and looking back between your legs, with your head as near to the ground as possible, you can see the top of the tree. The tree will be about the same height as the distance you have walked away from it.

 ## How old?

Ask children how you can work out the age of a tree, and sooner or later they will come up with the idea of counting the rings. One problem with that method is that you obviously can't use it with a living, standing tree.

Find a big old oak tree. You can estimate its age by measuring its girth, about 1.5 metres up from the ground. This can be done with a tape measure or a piece of string or, best of all, by seeing how many children it takes to encircle the tree, fingertip to fingertip with arms outstretched. You then estimate the girth by getting the children to stand in a line, fingertip to fingertip, and measuring them. You can bring some numeracy into this activity.

Use this table to convert centimetres to years:

Centimetres of girth	Estimated age of tree
185	80
250	100
300	140
370	180
430	230
500	300
560	370
620	430
680	520
750	600
800	700
930	930
1000	1000

BASED ON WOODLAND TRUST DATA

When you have worked out the rough age of your oak tree, ask the children to think about what was going on in history when the tree was beginning to grow, and all of the events that it has lived through. If you find an oak with a girth of 450cm or more, visit www.ancient-tree-hunt.org.uk and tell the Woodland Trust about it.

Further from home: tropical rainforests

If you thought our ancient woods were good for wildlife, you should see and hear a tropical rainforest. Here, the trees can be 50m tall, it is hot all year round and there is plenty of rain: some forests get over two centimetres of rain every day. Their name is a clue to where you find them: tropical rainforests are found in the tropics. South-east Asia, Africa and Central and South America all have them, and South America's Amazon is the biggest of the lot.

It's not always obvious if you visit one, but rainforests are heaving with life. There are more than 2000 bird species living in the Brazilian Amazon, out of a global total of about 10,000. Most of the world's beetles live in rainforests, the giant of which is Africa's Goliath beetle. At 110g it's a heavyweight: that's a lot for a beetle. The Bornean stick insect is another record-breaker to look out for. This is the world's longest insect and can be an impressive 50cm long.

Rainforests are home to reptiles, amphibians, fish, mammals, birds and many, many invertebrates. Over half of the planet's known animal and plant species live in rainforests. They are biodiversity hotspots, with all that variety packed into a habitat that occupies less than two per cent of the planet's surface.

Rainforest trees provide us with wonderful woods and delicious food. They include high-quality timber trees such as ebony, rosewood and mahogany, rubber trees and brazil nut trees. Rainforests are the natural home of pineapples, coconuts, bananas, avocados, coffee and cacao. Without cacao there would be no chocolate!

The rainforest is a natural medicine chest, too. The rosy periwinkle is used to treat leukaemia in children. Quinine is used to treat malaria: this comes from the bark of the *Cinchona* tree. The rainforest's medicinal qualities are not limited to a handful of species. A quarter of our medicines have their roots in the rainforest, and there could be 2000 tropical plants that might help us fight cancer.

Rainforests help us breathe. They soak up carbon dioxide, which helps to limit the effects of climate change, and release oxygen. Where would we be without oxygen?

Despite all that, in our shortsightedness we are destroying the world's rainforests. Why are we doing it? Here are some of the reasons:

- We're doing it to get timber: trees are cut down and shipped overseas to make expensive furniture.
- We're doing it to clear land for farms and plantations.
- We're doing it to grow oil palm, soy beans and sugar cane, which can be turned into biofuel as an alternative to petrol. That sounds good but it's wrecking the rainforest. Palm oil is also found in soaps, cosmetics and lots of processed foods, but large areas of forest have been cleared to produce it.
- We're doing it to build roads—across the Amazon rainforest, for example.
- We're doing it to mine aluminium and iron. Lots of these metals can be found in the ground beneath the Amazon rainforest.
- We're doing it by our contribution to climate change. Some areas of rainforest are drought-stricken and dying.

Rainforests provide us with food, medicines, timber and oxygen. That's reason enough to protect them. For the Christian, they tell us something about God and are an expression of his creative genius. They are part of the planet that God has asked us to look after.

Fresh cacao

Mangrove

Reproduced with permission from *Wow! Our Amazing Planet* by David Chandler (Barnabas in Schools, 2013) **www.barnabasinschools.org.uk**

What can we do?

It's difficult to do something practical for rainforests when you live in the UK. But here are some ideas:

- Support organisations that are actively involved in rainforest conservation. Take a look at www.rainforestconcern.org. A Rocha works with rainforests in Brazil and Peru, and you could support that work (www.arocha.org). The RSPB is working to save rainforest in Sumatra (www.rspb.org.uk).
- Spread the word. Persuade people that rainforests are wonderful places and need to be protected. Why not do an assembly with a rainforest theme? You could present it as part of a parents' evening.
- Use consumer power. Buy Brazil nuts. These can only be grown in the forest, not in plantations. If you are buying timber, furniture or paper products, look for FSC accreditation or something similar. The FSC logo is 'the mark of responsible forestry'. Look for products that have been certified by the Rainforest Alliance. (This is tricky for the children but easier if you can get their parents on board.)

Activities

Rainforest sounds

Find a recording of rainforest noises at night. Darken the classroom, use words to paint a picture of the forest, and get the children to listen in silence to the sounds of the forest. Then talk about the experience.

Rainforest collage

Create a tropical rainforest collage. This can be as big and colourful as you want to make it.

Rainforest animals

All of the animals below live in tropical rainforests, but which one lives where? Give the children the list of animals and ask them to match them to the right part of the world.

Animal	Part of the world
Jaguar	Central and South America
Mountain gorilla	Africa
Orang-utan	Borneo and Sumatra
Bengal tiger	India
Musky rat kangaroo	Australia

Forest dwellers

Ask the class to do some research, in pairs or small groups, about native people who live in the forest. What sort of buildings do they live in? Where does their food come from? What clothes do they wear? Will they be able to carry on living that way?

Troubled climate

Humankind's biggest impact on the natural world is our contribution to climate change. There is a layer of gases in our atmosphere that traps heat. This is called the greenhouse effect and is part of the way the world is designed to work. It's a bit like wrapping the world up in a duvet that keeps it at just the right temperature.

But things are hotting up. The world is getting warmer, and we are playing a part in making this happen. The gases that make up that 'duvet' include carbon dioxide and methane. Both of these are 'greenhouse gases'. Carbon dioxide is a byproduct of burning fossil fuels. We do this when we use coal or gas to make electricity, use petrol or diesel in our cars or take a trip on an aeroplane. Cleaning up water so that it is safe to drink, and pumping it to where we need it, also makes carbon dioxide. Methane is a smelly gas. When we make fertilisers we also make methane. When we grow rice we also make methane—and cows make it when they fart. These extra greenhouse gases trap more heat, like putting on a thicker duvet.

What that means is that the world is getting warmer. The ice at the north and south poles is melting. Sea levels are rising. Floods, droughts and hurricanes are happening more often. The climate is changing.

The effects are already being felt. There is a group of islands in the Pacific Ocean called Tuvalu. Less than 12,000 people live there, but they might not be able to do so for much longer. The February high tides are getting bigger. They come over the roads and into the farmland, and the seawater means that the land can't be farmed any more. There may come a time when the islanders will have to leave. If this happens, New Zealand has said that the islanders can go and live there. Fiji and the Cook Islands face the same problem. So do the Maldives in the Indian Ocean.

Many more people live in Bangladesh than in Tuvalu. The population of this Asian country is almost 150 million. Bangladesh is a low-lying country and there are floods every year. The monsoon can drop 50cm of rain in one day. Bangladesh is not a rich country, and it is the poorest people who will suffer most because of climate change. Their homes are on the lowest land, closer to the sea and alongside rivers. Seawater salt pollutes the soil and makes it hard to grow anything. In 2007 a big tropical storm hit Bangladesh and 3000 people died. As the climate changes, the effects could be even more severe. A 1.5m rise in the sea level would have an impact on 17 million Bangladeshis.

Elsewhere, glaciers are melting. A glacier is a river of ice that heads downhill very, very slowly. Higher temperatures would make the ice melt faster at the bottom of the glacier than it is being made at the top. It would look as if the glacier is heading back uphill. Take a look at these photos of the Upsala glacier in Argentina (also in the online gallery). The first one was taken in 1928. The second was taken in 2004, 76 years later. The difference is obvious and sobering.

Glacier, 1928

Glacier, 2004

Scientists predict that there will be many extinctions because of climate change. If an animal can't adapt quickly enough to changes to its environment, or move to a place where it can survive, its days are numbered. Plants are less mobile than animals. If they cannot adapt and their dispersal mechanisms are not able to relocate them to somewhere suitable, they are in trouble too.

Climate change is upon us, but we can take action to reduce its impact. There are some ideas for things you can do in the next section.

Activities

Discussion

Talk with your class about:

- Why it is better to use public transport than cars.
- Why countries need to work together on climate change.

Climate change video

There are video clips available that will help your class understand the realities of climate change and see what we can do to help. Here is one you could use as a starter: www.youtube.com/watch?v=QD2WTK94c1U

Start a climate change group

You will need a staff member or committed parent to make this work. The group could involve all interested children and meet at lunchtimes or after school. They can learn more about climate change in some fun ways and do something practical to make a difference.

Become an Eco-School

You can find out more at www.keepbritaintidy.org/EcoSchools (England), www.ecoschoolsscotland.org, www.eco-schoolswales.org or www.eco-schoolsni.org.

How does the greenhouse effect work?

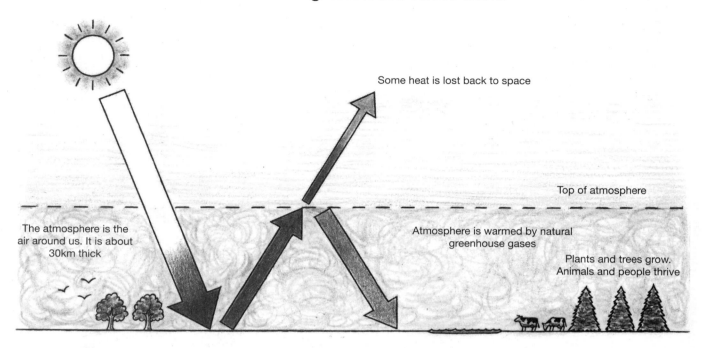

Some heat is lost back to space

Top of atmosphere

The atmosphere is the air around us. It is about 30km thick

Atmosphere is warmed by natural greenhouse gases

Plants and trees grow. Animals and people thrive

How are people changing the greenhouse effect?

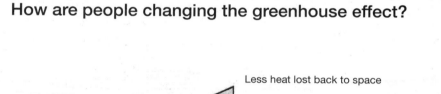

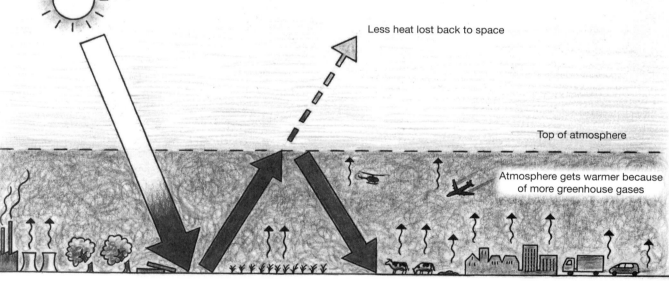

Less heat lost back to space

Top of atmosphere

Atmosphere gets warmer because of more greenhouse gases

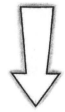

Climate change

Ice melts, sea levels rise
Extreme weather
Animals and plants affected

Who cares?

So far, we've made the case for creation being amazing, which it undoubtedly is.

We've taken a look at what the Bible has to say about creation, about our relationship with creation, and a bit about God's relationship with creation. We've told you about two Christians, passionate about the natural world—one of them historic (St Francis) and one contemporary (Dave Bookless). But despite the wonder of this world and our dependence on it, our track record of caring for it is flawed.

So what can be done, and who should be doing it? That's the focus of this section.

It's the government's job

The government makes the laws, and government ministers go to important international meetings and make agreements about the environment. It is not all down to them, but it is their job.

Most of the children in your class will have very little idea of what a government is and how it works. That's true of quite a few adults, too. These notes will help you give your class a basic understanding of what governments do.

What do governments do?

The UK is divided into smaller areas and each area has a Member of Parliament (MP). Adults vote to decide who the MP will be for their area. There are 650 MPs in our parliament. Most MPs belong to one of three political groups—Labour, Conservative or the Liberal Democrats. The different groups have different ideas about how things should be done. The group with the most MPs in parliament forms the government and it's the government's job to run the country. The person who leads the government is called the Prime Minister.

As well as the national government that runs the whole country, we have lots of local governments that look after much smaller areas. Adults vote to decide who will be in these, too. The people who get the most votes and win are called councillors.

Some issues, like climate change, affect the whole world. This means that governments from lots of different countries need to work together to agree on what should be done.

In 1992, a long time before any of the children in your class were born, there was a big, important meeting in Rio de Janeiro, a city in Brazil. Lots of people from lots of governments were there. They were trying to work out how we can all live on this planet without messing it up for people who will be alive in the future. There are more and more people living on the planet, so living this way gets harder and harder.

The meeting in Rio did make a difference. As a result of Rio, we're much better at recycling and don't bury as much of our rubbish in big holes in the ground. We couldn't have carried on doing that: we would have run out of space. They also thought that we should look after the world's wildlife. Our government made sure that we wrote a plan to help us do this. It included actions to take care of threatened plants, animals and habitats. There are local plans to help us do this, too.

There was another important meeting in 1997. This was before any of the children in your class were born, too. It was in Kyoto, Japan. At this meeting they talked about climate change and made a good decision: they decided to try to make less carbon dioxide, one of the greenhouse gases.

We all use electricity, which can be made by burning oil, coal and natural gas, but this releases carbon dioxide, so it makes climate change worse. The more electricity we can produce in ways that don't make carbon dioxide, the better. You might have seen wind farms—big, white wind turbines. These use the power of the wind to make electricity and don't make carbon dioxide. You might also have noticed that more and more people are putting solar panels on their roofs. These turn sunlight energy into electricity, and they don't make carbon dioxide either.

Cars that use petrol or diesel also make carbon dioxide. That's why it's good to walk, cycle or use the bus instead. Most buses do make carbon dioxide, but if there are lots of people on the bus it's less damaging than if all those people travelled in separate cars.

It might sound quite easy to sort these problems out, but it isn't. It's not easy to get lots of different countries to agree on what they should do about climate change. The world's rich countries have caused most of the problem. Some of the poorer countries want to get richer, but to do this often means making lots of carbon dioxide.

Activities

Prime Minister's question time

To help your class learn a bit more about the Prime Minister's job and what the government does, find out some interesting facts about the current Prime Minister. Tell them to your class and then encourage them to ask questions about what he does and what the government does. You could give the children some time to prepare some questions in advance.

Local councillors

Contact your local government and see if one of the councillors will come in to the school to answer questions from the children. The children will need to work out their questions before the event and may need some help with this. You could limit the questions to wildlife and the environment or range more widely.

I care!

Governments do try to help, but we can't leave it all to them.

Anyone who doesn't breathe is dead, and faith that doesn't do anything is just as dead! (James 2:26)

It isn't just the government's job. Everyone can do something to help. Christians should take seriously their responsibility to look after God's good creation. They haven't always been very good at that, but they are getting better. Some churches have become Eco-congregations. One of these is Christ Church at Davyhulme in Manchester. They run a project with the Energy Saving Trust and the local authority to encourage local people to insulate their homes, and they have offered insulation and grants for new boilers to 331 homes, saving 6000 tonnes of carbon dioxide.

Individuals can do things, too, and that includes the children in your class. Here are some suggestions of simple things that they can do to help:

- Put litter in the bin. It looks horrible if it's just left on the ground, and could be dangerous for wildlife. If it's rubbish that can be recycled, make sure that it ends up in the right bin.
- Don't waste water. Turn off the tap when you are brushing your teeth. Wildlife needs water, too. If we use too much, there is less for the wildlife. Wet wildlife places could dry out.
- Turn off lights if you don't need them on. Don't leave computers or TVs on if you don't need them. This saves money and, unless your electricity is made from a renewable source, cuts down on carbon dioxide production.
- Don't waste paper. Use both sides and reuse scrap paper if you can. When you buy a notebook or paper, buy one that is recycled or has the FSC logo (see page 68).
- Write to your MP or councillor. An MP doesn't need to receive many letters to take an issue seriously. Your children will need some guidance but, if there is an issue that they care about, why not help them write to the local MP or a local councillor about it? With support, even some Key Stage 1 students will be able to manage this.

There are quite a few activity ideas suggested on the following pages. Most of them focus on three key areas:

- Improving your school grounds for wildlife
- Climate change action
- Rubbish and waste: reduce, reuse, recycle

Improve school grounds for wildlife

There are lots of things you can do to make your school grounds better for wildlife. Even if you only have a tarmac playground, there are still things you can do. There is information about giving the birds food and water in Section 2 of this book, and on planting trees or a hedge in Section 4. Three different ideas are listed below. You don't have to do them all at once: just take your pick.

Activities

Make a minibeast home

This one is easy. All you need is twigs and some string. It works best if the twigs are all about the same length. Take a bundle of twigs, big enough to fill your hand, and tie it together with the string. You might need a piece of string around each end. Then find somewhere to put your bundle. You could tie it to a branch, push it into a fork on a bush or tree, or leave it on the ground under a bush. If you have the whole class making twig bundles, you might want to encourage some of the children to take them home and find a place for them there.

As a variation on this theme, fill a plastic tube or flowerpot with twigs, straw or even drinking straws cut to the right length. Put them in the same sorts of places as the twig bundles.

Make a minibeast mansion

You could do something on a much grander scale. You need a pile of wooden pallets or something similar. Fill the gaps with twigs, straw, soil, leaves, bricks with holes in them, bits of piping, wood with holes drilled, and anything else that might make a good minibeast home. (You might need the school caretaker's permission before you do this.)

Photo taken at RHS Garden Wisley

Reproduced with permission from *Wow! Our Amazing Planet* by David Chandler (Barnabas in Schools, 2013) **www.barnabasinschools.org.uk** 73

Make a nest box

(Key Stage 1 students will need lots of supervision for this activity.)

A nest box is a box that behaves like a hole in a tree. Blue tits and great tits often nest in them, especially if they can't find many trees with holes in them.

The children will need some help with this activity. The easiest way to involve your class is to pre-cut and pre-drill the wood so that they simply have to assemble it. Assess their abilities and decide how much of the construction it is realistic for them to do. See www.rspb.org.uk/Images/Nestbox%20pdf_tcm9-173857.pdf for a plan of a basic nest box.

- Your box doesn't have to be exactly the same size as the plan: the birds won't check it with a ruler!
- Don't use pressure-treated wood, as it's not good for the birds.
- Don't forget to drill some holes in the floor of the box. Then, if any water gets in, it can get out again.
- To help keep your baby birds safe, make sure the hole on the front is 12.5cm (or more) off the floor. That makes it hard for any marauding cats to take the birds out.
- You'll need a hinge for the lid. Ask a bike shop for a piece of old inner tube that you can cut up.
- You don't need to paint your box with anything: untreated timber is fine.

What size hole?

The size of hole you make will depend on which birds you want to attract. Big birds can't get into small holes.

Diameter of hole (mm)	What birds does it work for?
25	Blue tit, coal tit
28	Great tit
32	House sparrow

Some birds use boxes with half the front missing. For this sort of box, make the front piece of wood 10–14cm high. These boxes are good for wrens, robins and pied wagtails.

Where do I put the box?

If your box has a round hole in it, put it on a tree or wall. It should be two to four metres off the ground. Place it out of bright sunshine and in a position where rain won't blow in through the hole. You can use wire to fix a box to a tree. (Put the wire inside some old hosepipe

to protect the tree.) If you have made a box for house sparrows, fix it to a wall just below the roof.

If your box has half its front missing, you need to hide it low down (less than two metres up), in lots of plant cover. A wall covered in ivy would do the job well.

Cleaning the box

Don't spring-clean your box. Do an autumn clean instead. You'll need to make sure the birds have finished using the box, so don't clean it before August. Take out the old nest, scrape out any other bits and pieces, wash the box out with hot water, then let it dry.

Box cameras

You can buy nest boxes with cameras in them, and cameras to put in nest boxes. If you are able to do this, it will provide a great insight into life in the box.

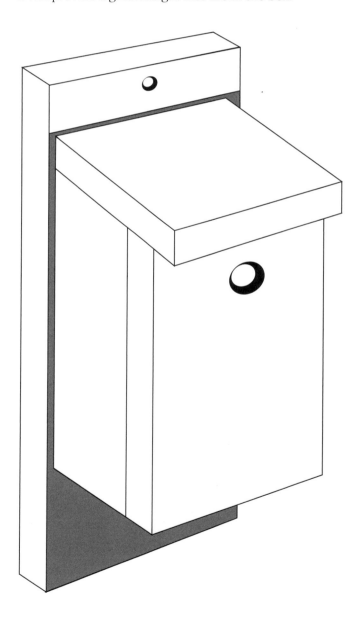

Take action for climate change

Climate change can be a daunting issue, but things can be done to reduce the amount of carbon dioxide we produce. Some of these suggestions are relatively simple to implement; some will need more effort and commitment. Don't feel guilty about what you haven't done. Do something—then, when you are ready, move on to the next idea.

Activity

  Climate change action plan

Think about things that you and the children can do at home, and things that you can do at school. The children will need parental support for some of the home activities, so tread carefully. You could work with the children to develop a school climate change action plan. For this to have maximum impact, you will need to get the support of senior management to make significant changes.

The information below might help. It looks at three areas for climate change action: energy, transport and shopping.

Energy

- The most obvious action is to switch electrical items off when you don't need them, and not to leave them on standby. A poster campaign and small reminder notes on or near light switches and computers may help everyone to remember.
- Think about turning the heating down a bit and wearing something warmer to save energy during the colder months. (Regulations may make this tricky at school.)
- If you are buying new electrical goods, check their energy rating and get the best you can afford.
- Consider changing your electricity supplier. There are two suppliers who provide only renewable energy: Good Energy (www.goodenergy.co.uk) and Ecotricity (www.ecotricity.co.uk). Switch to these and all the electricity you buy will have come from a renewable source. This is a very simple thing to do, which can make a big impact on your emissions.
- Make your own energy. Consider installing photovoltaic panels or other technologies that will make it possible for you to generate your own renewable electricity.

Transport

- Walk or cycle rather than using a car. If necessary, try to make walking to school a safer option for your children. A regular 'walking bus' may be a good idea. You may need to provide bike racks for children who cycle to school. Consider providing recognised safe cycling training for your pupils.
- Think about the transport you use on school trips. A coach is better than cars, but think about using public transport too. The journey itself will be a learning experience.
- Consider offsetting any carbon-making miles you travel. This involves making a donation to a scheme that will offset the carbon that resulted from your journey—by planting trees or providing fuel-efficient stoves for a developing country, for example. A Rocha runs an offsetting scheme called Climate Stewards. You can find out more at www.climatestewards.net.

Shopping

- Making things takes energy, and so does shipping them around the world. Normally, that means making carbon dioxide—in the factory or in transporting the goods. It may be difficult but try not to buy too many things that you don't really need. Charity shops are a useful option. You can get good-quality items there at a relatively low price. Reusing things like this is very sound environmentally and your money will go to a good cause.
- As much as possible, buy food that has been grown or produced locally. You could take a look at the catering policy that applies to your school: there may well be room for improvement. If you want to tackle this issue, you will need to think out your plan of action very carefully.
- Put your shopping in a reusable bag instead of getting a new carrier bag every time.

Rubbish and waste: reduce, reuse, recycle

Why do we want less rubbish? The things we throw away take energy and raw materials to replace. Having fewer things means that less energy is used in making them, which will make limited resources go further.

When we throw something away, it has to go somewhere. A lot of rubbish is buried in landfill sites, but this can't go on for ever. Landfill sites pollute the land and produce methane, a potent greenhouse gas. Rubbish can be a hazard to wildlife.

Most people are familiar with the 'reduce, reuse, recycle' mantra. The idea is that we should reduce the number of things we buy in the first place; reuse things rather than throwing them away (we might have to repair them first); and, if we have to throw something away, it should be recycled where possible, which includes composting garden and food waste.

Activities

  ### Nice and nasty

Use pictures of littered places in your own local area as a stimulus to discuss how rubbish makes children feel. Do they like what they see? How does it make them feel about these places?

Provide two copies of a rubbish-free scene, either a natural landscape or an urban setting, to children working in pairs. Ask the children to draw pictures of items of rubbish to stick on to one of the pictures. When the job is done, ask each pair to show their pictures to the rest of the group and to describe how they feel about the two contrasting scenes.

  ### Rubbish relay

You will need rubbish relay lists (one list per team). You might want to create your own list to match the rubbish items that you are able to collect, but examples might be:

- A red mesh fruit bag
- A yoghurt pot
- A cardboard tube
- A plastic bottle
- A sheet of newspaper
- Plastic wrapping

You will also need matching items of rubbish for each team (one item for each team member), one carrier bag per team, and space to run around in.

Line up the teams at one end of the open space and scatter the items of rubbish at the other. Give each team a copy of the rubbish relay list. Make sure they understand it before they start running. Each team member runs to the rubbish, chooses an item of rubbish, runs back to their team and puts the rubbish in the bag. Then the next team member runs. The first team to get one of each item of rubbish into the bag is the winner.

Add in adult helpers or ask children to run twice if you need to make up the numbers in any of the teams.

Which of these items could be recycled? Are there any that weren't needed in the first place?

  ## How long does it last?

Divide the class into teams. Give each team paper and pens or pencils. Read out the following list of items and ask the children to guess how long each item takes to decompose.

Paper	6 weeks
Orange peel	Up to 2 years
Newspapers	2–6 years
Plastic bags	10–20 years
Tin cans	100 years
Aluminium cans	200–500 years
Plastic fourpack holder	450 years
Wine bottle/glass jar	1 million years
Polystyrene	Never

Think about the varying impacts of throwing these things away. Highlight the importance of reducing, reusing and recycling.

  ## Where does it go?

This is a simple runaround quiz. Group the children in the middle of an open space. They need four places to run to, each with a different label:

- Compost it
- Recycle it at home
- Bin it
- Take it to the recycling centre

You may need different signs, depending on recycling arrangements in your area.

Call out a waste item. There's a list below to give you some ideas, but you can make up your own. The children run to the sign that they think is the right thing to do with that item. Reveal the right answer and tell them why it's correct. The children then return to the centre and you call out another item.

You might need to limit the amount of time they have to make their decision so that the game keeps moving. Counting down from five is one way to do this.

- Food waste
- Broken bricks
- Plastic bottles
- Scrap paper
- Teabags
- Leaves
- Tin cans
- Bits of wood (left over from DIY projects)
- Plastic food tubs
- Grass
- Magazines
- Old shoes
- Aluminium cans
- Glass bottles
- Cardboard
- Newspaper
- Foil
- Plastic food wrapping
- Disposable nappies
- Drinks cartons
- Carrier bags
- Oil
- Large garden waste (for example, branches)
- Batteries

 Green assembly

Help your class to organise a school assembly on a green theme. We have provided two PowerPoint presentations that might help (visit www.barnabasinschools.org.uk/ 9780857462497/):

- Recycled products: All sorts of things can be turned into something else. This short presentation shows pictures of a range of products. The audience have to guess what they were made from. The answers are included in the presentation.
- The journey of rubbish: This short presentation tells the story of what happens to our rubbish after we put it in the bin. It finishes with a reminder to 'reduce, reuse, recycle'.

Reducing and reusing

Talk about what 'reduce' actually means. It means 'to make smaller or make less'. Show the group a range of packaging that we throw away. Ask the children why we use it. Some packaging is necessary, but ask the group if they have any ideas for ways of reducing the amount of packaging that is used. When we do have packaging to dispose of, what's the best thing to do with it? (It depends what it is, of course.)

Activities

  Packed lunch game

Divide the group into teams of five. This game is a simple relay in which each team has to put together a packed lunch from a range of items. They run, choose an item, bring it back, and then the next team member runs.

Give them the following list so that they know what they have to collect:

- Something to put your lunch in
- A drink
- Some sandwiches
- A piece of fruit
- A treat

For each category, provide the following options:

- Something to put their lunch in (a reusable lunch box/bag or a throwaway bag)
- A drink (in a reusable bottle or a throwaway carton)
- Sandwiches (wrapped in clingfilm or in a reusable sandwich box)
- Fruit (a box of raisins or an apple)
- A treat (something home-made in a reusable container or something wrapped in lots of packaging)

Give different teams different tasks. Ask some to put together a lunch that makes as little waste as possible. Ask others to put together a really wasteful lunch. When they have completed their lunch boxes, each team explains why they made the choices they made.

Use the game as an introduction to a discussion about what goes into real lunch boxes. Ask the children if their lunches could be made any different. If so, ask them to choose one thing to try to do differently. This needs to be handled carefully: talk to them about how they might ask their parents about it.

As an extension, you could talk about food miles and make the link to climate change.

Get creative

Craft activities are a good way of reusing things. You could try the following:

- Paint glass jars. Give each child a glass jar and a piece of paper cut so that it wraps around inside the jar. First, draw and colour the design on the piece of paper. Then put the paper in the jar and use it as a guide to paint the outside with glass paints.
- Make cards from old cards and other 'rubbish'. (Did you know that the inside of some tetrapaks is shiny silver?)

Recycling

Talk with your class about why recycling is a good idea. Ask them to name five things (Key Stage 1) or ten things (Key Stage 2) that can be recycled at home, and five or ten things that can be recycled at school. If you are not already recycling these things, think about your reasons and come up with a plan so that you can recycle them.

Activities

  ## Recycling collage

Make a big collage using a whole host of materials that can be recycled. This could include a recycling message.

 ## A deeper understanding

Help your class to work out what happens to paper, glass and plastic cups when they are recycled. You might be able to arrange a visit to a local recycling facility to see how it's done.

  ## Greening your school

Photocopy or print the illustration on page 81 and give the copies out to the children. Ask the children to colour them in and to discuss what they see in the picture with a partner. Ask them if there is anything in the picture that you could do at your school.

Reduce Word Search

The words may run horizontally or vertically.

```
F  L  C  C  U  B  W  U  L  L  S
R  I  L  I  T  T  E  R  T  P  A
W  R  A  P  P  I  N  G  Y  A  E
G  E  N  L  R  L  A  A  R  C  I
T  D  D  R  U  P  G  P  R  K  I
T  U  F  Y  B  L  I  C  E  A  C
E  C  I  A  B  A  U  U  U  G  Y
C  E  L  I  I  S  L  S  S  I  L
P  O  L  Y  S  T  Y  R  E  N  E
C  T  E  G  H  I  E  R  T  G  A
I  R  E  C  Y  C  L  E  E  C  F
```

PACKAGING   RUBBISH   LANDFILL

WRAPPING   PLASTIC   POLYSTYRENE

LITTER   REDUCE   REUSE

RECYCLE

This wordsearch can also be downloaded at www.barnabasinschools.org.uk/9780857462497/

Reduce Word Search

Difficult!

The words may run backwards or forwards, horizontally, vertically or diagonally.

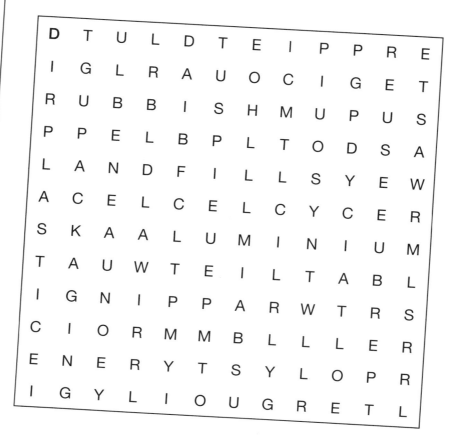

D	T	U	L	D	T	E	I	P	P	R	E
I	G	L	R	A	U	O	C	I	G	E	T
R	U	B	B	I	S	H	M	U	P	U	S
P	P	E	L	B	P	L	T	O	D	S	A
L	A	N	D	F	I	L	L	S	Y	E	W
A	C	E	L	C	E	L	C	Y	C	E	R
S	K	A	A	L	U	M	I	N	I	U	M
T	A	U	W	T	E	I	L	T	A	B	L
I	G	N	I	P	P	A	R	W	T	R	S
C	I	O	R	M	M	B	L	L	E	R
E	N	E	R	Y	T	S	Y	L	O	P	R
I	G	Y	L	I	O	U	G	R	E	T	L

PACKAGING   WRAPPING   LITTER

RECYCLE   RUBBISH   PLASTIC

ALUMINIUM   LANDFILL   POLYSTYRENE

REUSE   WASTE   POLLUTION

This wordsearch can also be downloaded at www.barnabasinschools.org.uk/9780857462497/

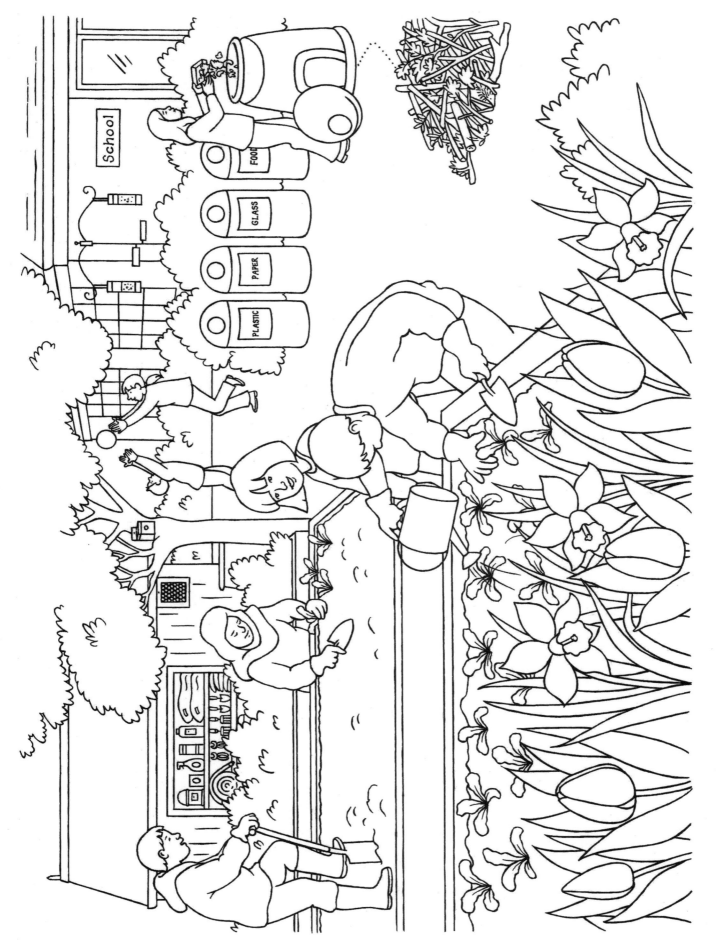

Is there hope for our world?

There is definitely hope for our world! The Christian message is one of hope.

Perhaps the most famous verse in the Bible is found in John's Gospel. John 3:16 says, 'For God so loved the world that he gave his one and only Son, that whoever believes in him shall not perish but have eternal life' (NIV).

Notice that it says, 'God loved the *world*'. Often, when this verse is quoted, it's understood to mean that God loved the *people* of the world. The theologians aren't sure what it means, but the original version uses the Greek word *kosmos*, which is where we get 'cosmos' from.

Most people understand the heart of the Christian message to be that Jesus died on the cross and rose from the dead so that our sins could be forgiven and we could have a relationship with God. But look at what the apostle Paul said when he wrote to the church in Colosse. He was writing about Jesus: 'Everything was created through him and for him... he holds all creation together... He made peace with *everything in heaven and on earth* by means of Christ's blood on the cross' (Colossians 1:16–17, 20, NLT, emphasis added).

This means that one day God will sort everything out and heaven and earth will be just how he wants them. That's something to look forward to! So, yes, there is hope. Paul is saying that what Jesus did on the cross is much, much bigger than many Christians realise.

It doesn't mean, though, that we can just sit back and wait for God to put everything right. The first commandment was that people should look after creation. There are Christians who are doing just that, and there are also non-Christians who are doing great things to look after the natural world.

This section includes some good, positive success stories—stories from A Rocha and stories from other conservation organisations. These are stories that give us hope. There are some activity ideas, too.

Success stories

The red kite

If you'd walked the streets of London in William Shakespeare's day, you would have had a very good chance of seeing a red kite. This magnificent bird of prey was a common scavenger in the capital, but London cleaned up its act, and this meant the end of the red kite in the city. The last recorded sighting in London was in 1859.

Red kite persecution started in the 16th century and was still going on in the 20th century. By the early 1900s, this bird was in serious trouble. It was almost extinct in Britain. One of the threats came from egg collectors, and the fact that the bird was rare only added to the desirability of its eggs. By the 1980s the red kite was globally threatened. Some still hung on in mid-Wales, but the future was looking bleak for this bird of prey. The birds were not in the best habitat, some were poisoned and others were lost to egg collectors.

The response to this dire situation has proved to be a great success. Working together, the RSPB and the government's conservation body initiated a reintroduction programme. In 1989, the first birds were brought to a site in southern England and a site in northern Scotland. The reintroduction continued until 1994, with most of the 'new' red kites coming from Sweden and Spain. In 1992, red kites bred at both reintroduction sites for the first time.

The programme has continued, with red kite releases in the East Midlands, central Scotland, Yorkshire, Dumfries and Galloway, north-east England, Northern Ireland and the Irish Republic. Red kites still have to contend with poisons put out for other creatures, and they sometimes fly into power lines, but there are now 1800–2000 pairs breeding in the UK. In some parts of the country they are very easy to see. Try driving along the M40, for example, through the Chilterns. Aston Rowant nature reserve between Junctions 5 and 6 is particularly good. In 2006, a red kite was seen in Hackney, London. The future is looking much brighter for this fabulous bird of prey with a long forked tail.

Minet Country Park

Southall and Hayes are on the north-western edge of London (see the map on page 88). They are not far from Heathrow Airport and are home to people of many south Asian nationalities, and refugees and asylum seekers from Sri Lanka, Kosovo and Somalia.

Somehow, a big area of land between Southall and Hayes had escaped developers. It had been abused for many years but was still home to wildlife. There were old oak trees that had once been part of hedgerows, there were streams, and sometimes kingfishers were seen. Twenty species of butterfly were identified, along with frogs, newts and even some nationally scarce water beetles. Burnt-out cars had been abandoned on the site and and there was lots of dumped rubbish. Local people referred to the area as the Minet Tip.

Remember Dave Bookless (St Dave in Section 3)? Dave noticed this area in 1998. He and his wife Anne had a vision that it could be cleaned up and transformed into a place that was good for people and for wildlife. There were challenges along the way—at one point it looked as if the site might become a football stadium

instead—but Dave and Anne worked with the local council and the local MP, local Christians prayed and wrote to councillors, and plans for the country park were approved.

From 2001 to 2003, Minet Tip was cleaned up and relandscaped using soil from the old Wembley stadium. Local people helped out at working parties, thousands of trees were planted, and eventually, after a lot of hard work, the transformed site was opened as Minet Country Park.

Hillingdon Borough Council owns the country park, but it wouldn't exist without A Rocha. A Rocha's work here has inspired other local projects, including a very successful interfaith allotment initiative.

Take a look at *Transformation*, a video that tells the Minet story (7 minutes 43 seconds). It can be found at www.arocha.org/int-en/resources/videos/5162-DSY.htm.

The otter

Otters have been through tough times. They've been killed for their beautiful fur, because they eat fish, and just for fun. They were also hit very hard by pollution and habitat loss in the 1950s and 1960s, to the extent that, by the 1970s, England had almost lost its otters. Otters need clean water, and our waterways were not very clean.

Chemicals used by farmers were dissolved by the rain and ended up in the rivers. This killed the fish, so there was less food available for the hungry otters. It also meant that otters died when they ate the poisoned fish. The good news is that many of those chemicals are illegal now. A lot of effort has gone into improving the state of our rivers, and otters have good legal protection.

Otters are doing well. They have been reintroduced to some areas and have found their own way back into others. In 2011, otters were seen in Kent, the last gap on the English map. They have made a comeback in every single English county, and they can also be seen in Scotland, Wales and Northern Ireland.

The Large Blue

The Large Blue butterfly is an insect that can be seen in much of Europe. Unfertilised, south-facing slopes where sheep graze are good Large Blue habitat. Starting in the 1800s, grazing patterns changed, leading to the Large Blue's disappearance from the British butterfly list back in 1979. But this is a success story.

The Large Blue has one of the strangest lifecycles of any butterfly. Without a red ant called *Myrmica sabuleti*, there would be few Large Blues. Its pink caterpillars eat wild thyme flowers. When a caterpillar has moulted as often as necessary (caterpillars have to moult to grow), it hurls itself to the ground and hides. It does this in the early evening because that is when the ants are out looking for food.

When all goes well, an ant finds the caterpillar and gives it a tap. This makes a special gland on the caterpillar, its 'honey gland', secrete a tiny drop of sweet fluid. The tapping continues and fellow ants are brought to the caterpillar. They 'milk' the caterpillar for a while, then head off—all except the ant that first found it. After more milking, the caterpillar does a very convincing impression of an ant grub: it lifts its body and changes its shape, giving it the tautness of an ant grub. It smells like one, too! The ant falls for the trick, grabs the 'grub' and takes it back to the nest.

In its new home, the caterpillar is surrounded by pre-packed food—ant grubs. One caterpillar might eat 1200 of them during its time in the nest. It gets fatter and hibernates, looking like a big white grub, and starts eating again in the spring. It's almost June before the big, fat caterpillar turns into a cocoon (it's possible that some Large Blues are in the ants' nest for two years before becoming a cocoon). The new butterfly takes to the air in June. Other ant species adopt Large Blue caterpillars, too, but many more caterpillars reach adulthood if they are found by the right species of ant. It's a fantastic lifecycle.

Reintroduction work began in 1983, using Large Blues from Sweden. They were brought to sites that had been grazed in the right way and where the right ant species was flourishing. The project was an instant success and the work has moved on, reintroducing Large Blues to around 100 places in four different areas. Somerset's Polden Hills are the stronghold. Here, as well as the reintroductions, the butterflies have established colonies on their own. The Large Blue is still threatened, but this is a great success story.

There is a short video clip about Large Blues at www.bbc.co.uk/nature/life (1 minute 22 seconds).

A Rocha in India

A Rocha is working in 19 countries around the world, one of which is India, where A Rocha has helped to find a solution to a big problem—elephants. This work is based near the Bangerghatta National Park, near Bangalore in the south of India (see the map on page 88). Elephants are protected in the national parks, but of course they can't read the signs and sometimes wander on to nearby farms, tempted by the tasty crops that the farmers are growing. Not surprisingly, the farmers are not happy about this. Sadly, elephants have been shot and killed, and have been known to trample people to death.

A wonderful solution has been found. Many deterrents were tried, but the most successful was chilli and tobacco. Elephants don't like the smell. To keep the elephants out, ropes are soaked in a mixture of oil, chilli and tobacco and hung around the edges of the farms. The elephants stay off the land, the farmers are happy, and the elephants are safer too.

Asian elephants

You could use the following elephant facts to put together a quiz.

- An elephant can live to be 70 years old, or older.
- There are three species of elephant in the world—two in Africa (the savanna elephant and the forest elephant) and one in Asia (the Asian elephant).
- Elephants have the largest brains of any animal. A male's brain is a bit bigger than a female's. It weighs five kilograms.
- Elephants' ears help them to stay cool. Warm blood flows into them and loses heat before returning to the body.
- African elephants have 21 pairs of ribs, but Asian elephants only have 20.
- Elephants' tusks are very long teeth. They can grow to be very heavy. One tusk can weigh 60kg.
- An elephant's trunk is part nose and part upper lip. Sometimes an elephant will use its trunk as a snorkel.
- The females give birth to one calf every 2½ to 4 years, but they don't have their first calf until they are 13 or 14 years old. They can carry on having calves until they are about 50 years old.
- It takes nine months for a human baby to grow before it is born. An average elephant pregnancy lasts just over 20 months. Their pregnancies last longer when it's a male elephant growing inside them than when it's a female.
- Elephants cry if they give birth to a dead calf.
- Elephants really do have very good memories.
- Sometimes elephants play and sometimes they laugh.

African elephants

Reedbeds

The common reed is a grass species that can grow to heights of three metres. It finds its own way into lakes, ponds, estuaries and ditches, and extensive areas of reed are known as reedbeds. Traditionally, reeds were harvested for thatching. Nowadays, most reed for thatching is imported from other parts of Europe, but some British reed is still used. Many of our reedbeds have been drained for farming, and those near the sea in East Anglia may be lost to a rising sea because of climate change.

Reedbeds are important habitats for the bittern (a hard-to-see heron), the bearded tit (a bird with a moustache rather than a beard), the reed warbler (which builds impressive nests with reed stems for support), and the marsh harrier, a big bird of prey that soars with its wings in a shallow 'v' shape. They are also good habitats for European eels (see page 56), water voles (like Ratty from *Wind in the Willows*), glorious Swallowtail butterflies and some specialist reedbed moths. The caterpillars of the Reed Leopard and Fenn's Wainscot feed inside reed stems, and Fenn's Wainscot eats reed leaves, too.

The good news is that new reedbeds are being created. At Lakenheath Fen in Suffolk, the RSPB turned a big carrot field into a wetland, with marshes and reedbeds. Lots of birds are now breeding in the reedbeds. In Cambridgeshire, the RSPB is turning a quarry into a huge nature reserve. It's called Ouse Fen, and when it's finished it will include the UK's largest reedbed. Not far away, a partnership of the local Wildlife Trust, local government and government agencies is working together on 'The Great Fen', another large-scale project that will be putting reedbeds back into the landscape. Things are looking up for reedbeds and the wildlife that depends on them.

Sokoke and ASSETS

In Kenya, A Rocha is working to protect the Aruboko-Sokoke forest (see the map on page 88). This is the biggest remaining chunk of what used to be a huge coastal forest stretching from Mozambique all the way up to Somalia. The forest is especially important for two animals—the golden-rumped elephant shrew, which is only found in Kenya, and the Sokoke scops owl, which is found only in Kenya and Tanzania.

Despite the forest's legal protection, local people still cut down the trees and hunt its animals. In Kenya, high school education has to be paid for, and cutting down trees provides a way to pay the school fees.

A Rocha came up with a great solution. It's called ASSETS—the Aruboko-Sokoke Schools and Ecotourism Scheme. Rich visitors from overseas go there to see the wildlife. A Rocha are charging them for the privilege and getting them to help with conservation work during their visit. Local people are working as guides and building hides for wildlife watching, and walkways. With the money that ASSETS has raised, A Rocha provides bursaries so that local children can go to high school. It's a win–win–win situation: the forest is doing better, the children are being educated and the local people are getting work.

The Sokoke scops owl

This little owl was discovered in Kenya in 1965. It is just 15–18cm long. It eats invertebrates and is active at night, as well as dusk and dawn.

Golden-rumped elephant shrew

This is a big shrew. From the tip of its tail to the tip of its nose, it measures 44–49cm. It eats invertebrates, including earthworms and millipedes. Despite its name, it is more closely related to the elephants than the shrews.

India

Bangalore

Aruboko-Sokoke Forest

Kenya

Tanzania

London

Activities

  Make an elephant mask

- Photocopy the template below, or download from www.barnabasinschools.org.uk/9780857462497/. Use thin card to make multiple copies.
- Children should colour the mask in appropriate felt-tip colours.

- Cut out the mask shape and the eyeholes. Young children may need help with one or both of these tasks.
- Make a small hole with a pencil at either edge of the mask, near the eyes.
- Thread some fine elastic through the holes and knot at either end so that the mask will fit comfortably around the child's head.

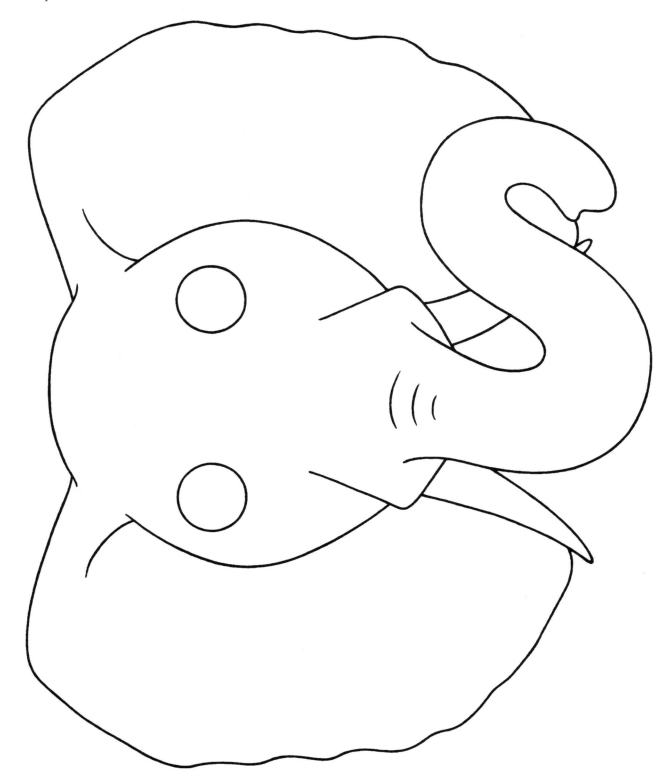

The Bible and creation care

Explain to another class, or to parents at an assembly or open evening, what the Bible says about looking after the world. Then tell them five things that we can do to help.

 ## Sokoke species research

Find out more about the golden-rumped elephant shrew and the Sokoke scops owl. Tell someone what you find out.

 ## Success stories

Use books or the internet to find out about other 'wild success' stories. Prepare a two-minute presentation to show to the rest of your class.

  ## A Rocha fund-raising

Why not raise some money for an A Rocha project? The work in India and ASSETS in Kenya are good ones, but there are others: you can find out more at www.arocha.org.

Further resources

Printed resources for children

Natural history

- Mike Unwin, Sarah Whittley and Rachel Lockwood, *RSPB My First Book of Garden Birds* (A&C Black, 2006)
- Anita Ganeri and David Chandler, *RSPB First Book of Birds* (A&C Black, 2011)
- David Chandler and Mike Unwin, *RSPB Children's Guide to Bird Watching* (A&C Black, 2007)
- Mike Unwin, *RSPB My First Book of Garden Bugs* (A&C Black, 2009)
- Anita Ganeri and David Chandler, *RSPB First Book of Minibeasts* (A&C Black, 2011)
- David Chandler, *All About Bugs* (New Holland, 2008)
- David Chandler, *All About Garden Wildlife* (New Holland, 2008)
- Anne and John Bebbington, Steve Tilling and Countryside Council for Wales, *The Woodland Name Trail* (Field Studies Council, 2000) (a minibeast key on a fold-out chart)

Printed resources for adults

Natural history

- Simon Harrap, *RSPB Pocket Guide to British Birds* (A&C Black, 2nd edn 2012)
- Peter Holden and Tim Cleeves, *RSPB Handbook of British Birds* (A&C Black, 3rd edn 2010)
- Michael Chinery, *Insects of Britain and Western Europe* (A&C Black, 3rd edn 2012)
- Richard Lewington, *Pocket Guide to the Butterflies of Great Britain and Ireland* (British Wildlife Publishing, 2003)

Creation care

- Dave Bookless, *Planetwise* (IVP, 2008)
- Ruth Valerio, *'L' is for Lifestyle* (IVP, 2008)

Online resources

- The Ancient Tree Hunt: www.ancient-tree-hunt.org.uk
- Arkive: www.arkive.org (a 'multimedia guide to the world's endangered animals, plants and fungi')
- A Rocha: www.arocha.org
- www.arocha.org/int-en/resources/videos/5162-DSY.htm (the story of the Minet project)
- Buglife (the Invertebrate Conservation Trust): www.buglife.org.uk
- Ecoschools England: www.keepbritaintidy.org/EcoSchools
- Ecoschools Northern Ireland: www.eco-schoolsni.org
- Ecoschools Scotland: www.ecoschoolsscotland.org
- Ecoschools Wales: www.eco-schoolswales.org
- Ecotricity (electricity provider): www.ecotricity.co.uk
- Friends of the Earth: www.foe.co.uk
- Good Energy (electricity provider): www.goodenergy.co.uk
- The Good Fish Guide: www.goodfishguide.co.uk
- iSpot: www.ispot.org.uk (for help with identification)
- Nature Detectives: www.naturedetectives.org.uk (for lots of downloadable resources)
- Rainforest Concern: www.rainforestconcern.org
- The Royal Pigeon Racing Association: www.rpra.org
- The RSPB: www.rspb.org.uk
- The Sustainable Eel Group: www.sustainableeelgroup.com
- The Woodland Trust: www.woodlandtrust.org.uk
- *Wow! Our Amazing Planet* online resources: www.barnabasinschools.org.uk/9780857462497/

Answers to 'Name the bird' quiz on page 24

1.	Magpie	6.	Blackbird
2.	Sparrow	7.	Wren
3.	Carrion crow	8.	Wood pigeon
4.	Collared dove	9.	Starling
5.	Blue tit	10.	Robin

Barnabas RE Days

Exploring Christianity creatively

A Barnabas RE Day is a full day's visit to your school to bring the Bible to life for primary-aged children through a range of the creative arts. The Barnabas Children's Ministry team explores themes such as 'Whose world?', 'Who is my neighbour?', 'Who am I?', 'What's so special about the Bible?', 'It's not fair', Advent and Christmas, Lent and Easter, and Harvest, using Bible stories and contemporary life illustrations. The themes address many PSHE/Citizenship objectives. For example:

- *Whose world?* What improves or harms our environment; responsibility towards our environment.
- *Who is my neighbour?* Recognising choices; realising that other people have needs; caring; bullying; racism.
- *Who am I?* Recognising similarities and differences between people; feeling positive about ourselves; recognising our worth as individuals; recognising and challenging stereotypes.

The sessions use different creative arts according to the particular skills of the team member undertaking your booking, such as storytelling, music, dance, mime, drama, creative writing or drawing. The material is based on biblical and historical accounts, personal story and shared experience. The timetable, class groupings and themes are completely flexible and will be organised between you and the Barnabas ministry team to suit your school's needs.

A full-day visit costs just £275, of which £50 is placed down as a non-returnable deposit when booking.

For more information, contact the Barnabas Team Administrator on 01865 319704 or email barnabas@brf.org.uk. You can also visit the website: www.barnabasinschools.org.uk.

What schools have said about Barnabas RE Days:

A hugely inspirational day which really enthused our children—especially the assembly which appropriately engaged everyone. A request has been made that we have an RE week in school because our RE day was so successful.

Staff were unanimous in their view that it was an excellent day.

An excellent, informative day. The children enjoyed it immensely and can still remember aspects of their workshops now a month on!

Barnabas INSET

In addition to publishing resources and running RE Days in school for children, Barnabas also offers INSET sessions for teachers. An INSET session lasts two hours, with the option to run two sessions on one day, and follow-up material is available.

Following discussion with the Barnabas team coordinator and the individual Barnabas team member who will be leading the INSET, a session may combine elements from more than one of the following outlines.

- Using Drama in RE
- Storytelling and the Bible
- Collective Worship and Reflection
- Art and Spirituality
- Using the Bible with Children

There is also the opportunity to include within the INSET programme an element of 'Quiet Spaces', an enriching and enjoyable time for the staff to be still and reflect on wider questions than day-to-day teaching.

What schools have said about Barnabas INSET:

Thank you very much for a superb session... it was just what we needed, and I'm sure you realised from the comments as people left that it was very much appreciated by everyone there.

When I signed up for your RE INSET day I was looking for an easy day where the children would be inspired by the Bible, and your personality and the way you presented the Bible really inspired me.

It was inspirational, demonstrating how to make RE a fun interactive experience.

Christianity: Key Beliefs and Traditions

An RE resource for teaching Christianity at Key Stage 2

Cavan Wood

Christianity: Key Beliefs and Traditions is an essential resource for teaching Christianity at Key Stage 2. It seeks to inform and equip RE teachers by looking at key theological ideas such as creation and salvation as well as at the life of Jesus and the growth of the church.

Over 30 topics are covered, each including background information, classroom activities and learning objectives. The emphasis is not just on the history of Christianity but on the Christian faith as it is lived now and on evaluating its key ideas, linking themes to pupils' experience and understanding.

ISBN 978 0 85746 251 0   UK £7.99
Available direct from BRF: please visit www.brfonline.org.uk

Teaching Narnia

A cross-curricular classroom and assembly resource for RE teachers

Olivia Warburton

Drawing on C.S. Lewis's classic series, *Teaching Narnia* provides a wealth of creative and interactive ideas for use in the classroom and in collective worship. The Narnia books are an important part of Christian and literary heritage in the UK, with teaching applications beyond RE and Literacy to PSHE and Citizenship and a number of other curriculum areas. They help children to explore and develop their worldview, tackling big questions such as: What is really real? How do we see the world? Who is in charge of the world? Is God really good? Does he exist at all? What happens after death? and How do we know what is right and wrong?

This resource includes:

- background information about C.S. Lewis's life
- 15 lesson plans for use in the classroom
- a section of drama workshop activities
- assemblies and follow-up ideas for Christmas and Easter
- plot summaries of each book in the series

ISBN 978 0 85746 256 5   UK £6.99
Available direct from BRF: please visit www.brfonline.org.uk

Where in the World?

An RE and assembly resource on the worldwide Christian Church

Martyn Payne

Where in the World? is a global Christianity resource for primary school RE teachers. It provides lesson outlines, assembly material, a five-week scheme of work, background information and a section on learning objectives and outcomes. Content includes:

- A journey story focusing on seven churches around the world
- Background about the Christian faith in each of the countries visited
- The growth of the worldwide Christian Church
- How Christians worship and major festivals
- International Christians who have made a difference
- Guidance on making safe and successful global connections
- Prayers and songs from around the world
- A list of world anniversaries for themed days
- Links to further resources online
- Web material to download at www.barnabasinschools.org.uk/whereintheworld/

ISBN 978 0 85746 155 1   UK £9.99
Available direct from BRF: please visit www.brfonline.org.uk

Enjoyed
this book?

Write a review—we'd love to hear what you think. Email: reviews@brf.org.uk

Keep up to date—receive details of our new books as they happen.
Sign up for email news and select your interest groups at:
www.brfonline.org.uk/findoutmore/

Follow us on Twitter @brfonline

By post—to receive new title information by post (UK only), complete the form below and post to: BRF Mailing Lists, 15 The Chambers, Vineyard, Abingdon, Oxfordshire, OX14 3FE

Your Details
Name _____
Address_____
_____
Town/City _____ Post Code _____
Email _____

Your Interest Groups (*Please tick as appropriate)

- ❏ Advent/Lent
- ❏ Bible Reading & Study
- ❏ Children's Books
- ❏ Discipleship
- ❏ Leadership
- ❏ Messy Church
- ❏ Pastoral
- ❏ Prayer & Spirituality
- ❏ Resources for Children's Church
- ❏ Resources for Schools

Support your local bookshop
Ask about their new title information schemes.